THE
LANGUAGE
PEOPLE
REALLY
USE

LINGUISTICS FOR CANADIANS SERIES

General Editors: Michael Gregory, M.A.
Professor of English, Glendon College,
York University

Richard J. Handscombe, M.A.
Associate Professor and Chairman of the
English Department, Glendon College, York University

THE LANGUAGE PEOPLE REALLY USE

JAMES D. BENSON, Ph.D.
Assistant Professor of English, Glendon College,
York University

WILLIAM S. GREAVES, M.A.
Assistant Professor of English, Glendon College,
York University

THE BOOK SOCIETY OF CANADA LIMITED
Agincourt
Canada

© The Book Society of Canada Limited, 1973

Cover design by James H. Fairbairn
Diagrams by Steven R. Fernley and Brian B. Sheppard

ISBN 0-7725-5014-X

2 3 4 5 6 7 8 9 81 80 79 78 77 76 75

Printed in Canada

ACKNOWLEDGEMENTS

The Language People Really Use is the direct result of the special focus on language in the Glendon College English curriculum. The English department, composed both of linguists and of members trained in traditional approaches to literature, was formed under the direction of Professor Michael Gregory, whose article "Aspects of Varieties Differentiation" (*Journal of Linguistics*, 1967) provides the theoretical basis both of our first-year programme and of this book. The grammatical model we use is based on the Scale-and-Category theory of M.A.K. Halliday, and in particular upon Professor Gregory's *English Patterns*.

The book has benefited greatly from the rigorous criticism of our colleagues, who have been quick to point out faults and omissions, and generous in providing material that was wanting. In particular we want to thank Professor Peter Minkus, who guided our initial attempts at collecting a series of clearly marked texts; Professor David Clipsham, who stepped in and offered good advice at all stages of the book, and whose clear thinking was indispensable to the resolution of theoretical problems; and Professor Richard Handscombe, whose extensive knowledge of approaches to the teaching of English was invaluable. Welcome editorial assistance was provided by Brian Meeson, language consultant for the Toronto Board of Education.

J. D. B.
W. S. G.

We wish to thank the following authors (or their representatives) who have kindly permitted the reproduction of copyright material.

Addison-Wesley Publishing Company: *Advanced Calculus*, First Edition, 1952, by William Kaplan

Aerofin Corporation: Aerofin (Piping—Flexitube)

American Library Association: excerpt from "Preface" to *Guide to Reference Books*

The Atmospheric Environment Service of the Dep't. of the Environment, Government of Canada: Weather Map

Basic Books, Inc. Publishers: excerpt from "Sociology: Its Present Interests", by Harry Alpert, from Ch. 5, *The Behavioral Sciences Today*, ed. Bernard Berelson

Beaucraft Greeting Cards Ltd.: illustration

G. Bell & Sons, Ltd.: excerpt from "Introduction", *Latin Grammar*, 1951, by E.C. Marchant & G. Watson

The Bodley Head and the Estate of James Joyce: excerpt from *Ulysses*, by James Joyce

Bolivar Press, Kingston, W.I.: excerpt from *Children of Sisyphus*, by Orlando Patterson

The British Museum (Trustees of): excerpt from *Beowulf* (facsimile)

Canadian Broadcasting Corporation: excerpt from TV script adapted from Harold Pinter's drama *The Basement*

Jonathan Cape Ltd. and the Executors of the James Joyce Estate: excerpt from *A Portrait of the Artist as a Young Man*, by James Joyce

Center for Applied Linguistics, Washington, D.C.: excerpt from *Conversations in a Negro American Dialect*, by Bengt Loman

Chatto & Windus Ltd.: excerpt from "Lawrence Scholarship and Lawrence", *Anna Karenina and Other Essays*, by F.R. Leavis; excerpt from *D.H. Lawrence: Novelist*, by F.R. Leavis

Cinecity, Toronto: advertisement

Clarendon Press: excerpt from *The Earlier Tudors*, 1485-1558, by J.D. Mackie; excerpts from *The Lore and Language of Schoolchildren*, by Iona & Peter Opie

The Council of the Early English Text Society: transliteration, excerpt from *Beowulf* (facsimile)

Dual 1009 SK of United Audio Products Inc., Mount Vernon, N.Y.: Owner's Manual of Automatic Turntable

E.P. Dutton & Co., Inc.: excerpt from *The Pooh Perplex*, by Frederick C. Crews. Copyright © 1962 by Frederick C. Crews. Published by E.P. Dutton, Inc. in a paperback edition

Encyclopaedia Britannica Publications Ltd.: excerpt from "Abor Hills", *Encyclopaedia Britannica*, 11th edition, 1910-1911

Engraved Stationery Manufacturers' Association, Inc., Chicago: pp. 28, 29, *Proper Forms of Engraving for Social Use*, 1967 ed., by Mary Hunter

Evergreen Review, and Bernard Mazel: "Alive and Burning" (mailing piece)

Farrar, Straus & Giroux, Inc.: excerpt from *The Electric Kool Aid Acid Test*, Tom Wolfe

Faber & Faber Ltd.: excerpt from "The Love Song of J. Alfred Prufrock", *Collected Poems, 1909-1962*

Ginn and Company: excerpts from *New Latin Grammar*, ed. Greenough, Kittredge, Howard and D'Ooge. Copyright © 1903, renewed 1931

Government of Ontario, Dep't. of Information & Public Relations: pp. 1, 2 & 3, "Remarks of the Hon. William G. Davis, Committee on University Affairs, Upon the Introduction of the Estimates of the Dep't. of University Affairs for 1970-1"; pp. 7-9, "Remarks for Seminar on Student Power, the University and Society", the University of Western Ontario, Friday, 24th Jan., 1969, by D.T. Wright, Chairman, Committee on University Affairs

Harcourt Brace Jovanovich, Inc.: "nobody loses all the time", *Poems, 1923-54*, by e.e. cummings. Copyright 1926 by Horace Liveright; renewed 1954 by E.E. Cummings

Holt, Rinehart & Winston Ltd.: "Letter to Lord Bute", *Rasselas, Poems and Selected Prose* (Samuel Johnson), ed. Bertrand H. Bronson

Houghton Mifflin Company: excerpt from "A Treatise on the Astrolabe", *The Works of Geoffrey Chaucer*, ed. F.N. Robinson

Indiana University Press: pp. 218-221, *Animal Communication*, by Thomas A. Sebeok

Jenyon & Eckhardt Ltd.: Peter Dawson advertisement

Joan Daves, New York, Literary Agent: excerpt from a recording of "I Have a Dream", by Martin Luther King, Jr.

Methuen & Co. Ltd.: for excerpt of TV adaptation, *The Basement*, Harold Pinter; excerpt from *The Lover*, by Harold Pinter

Mitchell, W.O.: excerpt from CBC radio script "Jake and the Kid", Series V, Programme 7, Nov. 7, 1954

Molson's Brewery (Ontario) Limited: Molson Golden Ale radio commercial

Thomas Nelson, Inc.: p. 45 *Psychoanalysis*, by Clara Thompson

New Directions Publishing Corp.: excerpt from *The Selected Letters of Ezra Pound, 1907-1941*, ed. D.P. Page. Copyright 1950 by Ezra Pound

W.W. Norton & Company Inc.: excerpts from *Elizabethan Handwriting, 1500-1650*, Giles E. Dawson & Laetitia Kennedy-Skipton

Olivetti Canada Limited: advertisement

Ontario Dep't. of Trade & Development (Information Services): the beginning paragraphs of a speech by the Honourable Stanley J. Randall, Ontario Minister of Trade and Development (November 8th, 1963 – February 28th, 1971) to the Rotary Club of Toronto, February 19, 1971

Petersen-Hulme Limited, Toronto: Dubonnet advertisement

Random House, Inc.: excerpts from *As I Lay Dying*, by William Faulkner

Ray Torresan & Associates (International) Ltd., Montreal, and Macdonald Tobacco Marketing Ltd.: Export "A" advertisement

Redi-Set Business Forms, Toronto: memoranda sheets

Ringrone Newspapers, Cheltenham, Eng.: *Intelligence Digest Service* sheets

Scott, Foresman and Company: excerpt from *College Latin*, by de Witt, Gummere and Horn. Copyright 1954 by Scott, Foresman and Company

Charles Scribner's Sons: p. 62, *The Sun Also Rises*, by Ernest Hemingway. Copyright 1926, Charles Scribner's Sons; renewal copyright 1954, Ernest Hemingway

The Society of Authors, on behalf of the Bernard Shaw Estate: extract from *Pygmalion*, by Bernard Shaw

S.P.C.K. (The Society for Promoting Christian Knowledge): excerpt from *Thomas Ken: Bishop and Non-Juror*, by Hugh A.L. Rice

The Swallow Press Incorporated: "Rose", Tim Ulrichs; "U", Jiri Valch; "Elimination", Franz Vanderlinde; "Astrodome", Edwin Morgan; *Anthology of Concretism*, ed. Eugene Wildman. Copyright © 1969

The *Toronto Star* Syndicate: *Weather Report*, June 1, 1971; "Stars might be giants, but film isn't", Film Review, June 1, 1971

United States Government, Dep't. of Treasury, Internal Revenue Service: excerpt from 1970 Federal Income Tax Form

United States Government Printing Office: p. 268, "Winds", *American Practical Navigator*, Ch. XXI, 1943, by Nathaniel A. Bowditch

Wehr Corporation, Continental Air Filters: Media Installation, Form BO41

Dr. Williams's Library, London, Eng.: "Preface", by Rev. Roger Thomas, M.A., to *The Catalogue of Accessions*, 1900-1950

York University, Downsview, Ont.: p. 21, *Faculty of Arts and Science Calendar*, 1969-70

Every effort has been made to trace the owners of the copyright material that appears in this book. The publishers offer their apologies for any unintentional errors or omissions in the acknowledgments and will gladly make any corrections in subsequent editions.

CONTENTS

DIATYPIC ANALYSIS

PART THREE: DIALECTAL VARIETIES

PART FOUR: LITERATURE

GLOSSARY, pp. 195 - 202

INTRODUCTION

The Language People Really Use attempts three things: to bring together samples of language which does not normally make its way into the classroom, to provide a more adequate method of analysing these texts than the more traditional approaches, and to relate the analysis of such language to the study of literature.

The book is arranged in four sections. Part One introduces the concept of levels of language. Although linguists dispute the number and kinds of levels that can be abstracted from language, there is agreement that graphology/phonology, grammar, and lexis are three distinct levels of language and of linguistic description. We begin with a description of these three levels in order to establish clear and consistent criteria for the analysis of the varieties of English which follow.

Part Two is concerned with diatypic varieties of English — those different kinds of English we utter or write according to our varying situations and intentions.

Part Three illustrates briefly the dialectal varieties of English. Over these, the language user has far less control. Every speaker is tied to his own dialects — not only geographical dialect, but also social, temporal and personal dialects. A complete description of these dialects would involve a high degree of specialization. Our examples have been discussed in a relatively informal way.

Part Four illustrates the application of the varieties framework to the study of literature. This, we feel, makes a fitting conclusion to the book, because literature draws upon all the resources of language, and is consequently more complex than most non-literary varieties of English. The literature has been selected from a wide range of possibilities, and includes a speech and two letters as well as poetry and fiction.

There is a full glossary at the end of the book.

Part One

Levels of Language

— Graphology/Phonology
— Grammar
— Lexis

GRAPHOLOGY

The patterns of graphology, marks that carry meaning, *work* — or you couldn't read this paragraph. But how do they work? Many a driver can make a car work without ever looking under the hood. It can, however, be useful to know the relationship between distributor and spark plug. It could save you money! Similarly it can be useful — and it certainly is interesting — to know how graphic substance is organized.

Graphic substance — the letters, punctuation marks and other symbols in which a written language is expressed — can be produced by various means, and in different mediums: pen on paper, typewriter on paper, and type on paper are familiar examples. There are, of course, others, such as chisel on stone. Most of these share the characteristic of relative permanence. Nearly all of these are more permanent than speech, although some of the more exotic types, such as cathode ray on the surface of a television tube or CO_2 in the air (skywriting) are only marginally so.

We will be using the term "graphic resources" to refer to the mediums which can be utilized to produce graphic substance. The letter "A", which graphic resources (black ink, type-face, and paper) can produce, is part of the graphic substance of English. Black shading around a piece of writing, which might give it a particular effect, constitutes a *use* of graphic resources but, since it is not part of the language system, cannot properly be said to be part of the graphic substance of the language. The linguist, because he is interested in the effect of a piece of language, is interested in non-language features which are associated with it. He will, however, keep in mind the theoretical difference between graphic substance, which is a language feature, and any non-language utilization of graphic resources.

Graphology is closely related to, but quite distinct from, graphic substance. Graphology is the patterned way in which the graphic substance is related to the grammar and lexis of the language.

4

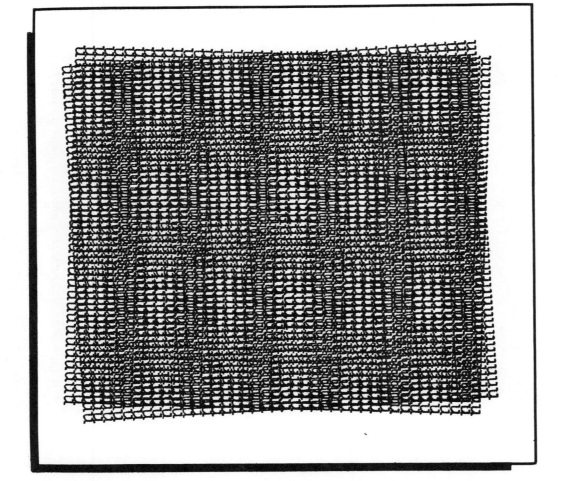

This concrete poem is language at one level only: graphology. The patterns shown here are language, in that they convey more meaning within an English-speaking community than they would in, say, an Arabic community. The main utilization of graphic substance, however, is a matter of design, and the "u" poem's appeal, or lack of appeal, to a particular group would depend on cultural considerations other than language.

Non-language design is obviously an important part of the "Elimination" poem also, but it stands within the general framework of English. The "Elimination" poem exists as language at three levels: lexis, grammar and graphology, and although it could not be completely translated to the spoken mode, more of it could be spoken than the "u" poem.

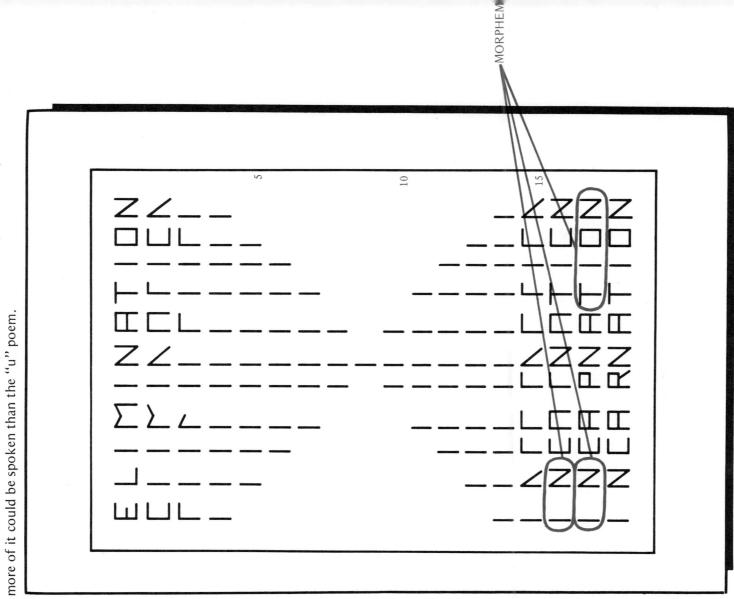

MORPHEM[E]

EXERCISE:

Discuss the way graphic resources are utilized in the "Elimination" poem. What is the relationship between graphic substance and visual design?

Design is important here, but the "rose" poem lies more within the domain of language than does the "Elimination" poem. There are, at the graphological level, no marks which are not clearly English letters, although the arrangement of these letters does not result in an entirely English text.

```
roseros    erose
roseroseroserose
roseroseroserose
roseroseroserose
roseroseroserose
roseroseroserose        5
roseroseroserose
roseroseroserose
roseroseroserose
roseroseroserose
roseroseroserose       10
eros
```

EXERCISES:

Two words emerge from this text: "rose", because it begins each line, and "eros", because it is isolated in the bottom line.

1. In what ways are these words related to each other?

2. The "Elimination" poem also uses two related words. Describe the different ways in which the utilization of graphic resources contributes to the meaning of the "Elimination" poem and the "rose" poem.

3. Pick two words that can be related to each other both in terms of meaning and in terms of the way they appear on the page ("eros" and "rose" are presented anagrammatically and "elimination" and "incarnation" are printed in such a way that they share eleven vertical lines). Try to write a concrete poem, arranging the words in such a way that the visual impact of the poem contributes effectively to the relationship of the words as words.

Visual design is present in "Astrodome", as it is in the "u" poem, the "Elimination" poem, and the "rose" poem, but it does not dominate our attention to the same extent because of the greater complexity of the language used. The relationship between visual design and language is still important, however. For example, printing the right-hand words as a distinct column places a strong emphasis on the words "glass" and "grass".

ASTRODOME

'As real grass withers in the Astrodome (at Houston,
Texas), it has been replaced by Astrograss.'

(news item)

```
all is not grass that astrograss
that astrograss is not all grass
that grass is not all astrograss
astrograss is not all that grass          5
is that astrograss not all glass
not all astrograss is that glass
all that glass is not astrograss
that is not all astrograss glass          10
that glass is not all fibreglass
not all that fibreglass is glass
fibreglass is not all that glass          15
is that not all fibreglass glass
that fibreglass is not all grass
glass is not all that fibreglass
is all astrograss not that glass          20
all is not grass that fibregrass
```

EXERCISES:

1. There are no capital letters or periods in "Astrodome". Are sentence boundaries indicated graphologically in any way? Does every sentence end at the end of a line? What difficulties arise when you try to punctuate the poem? Give specific examples.

2. Compare "Astrodome" with T.S. Eliot's "The Love Song of J. Alfred Prufrock", or any other poem of your choice, in terms of its *utilization* of graphic resources. Point out all the details you can — punctuation marks, use of capital letters, the shape of the printed poem on the page, the kind and size of type. In short, make any statement you can about the marks on the paper.

The basic function of a text's graphology is to transmit lexical and grammatical information to the reader. This text does more, however. The word "cinemascope" and the phrase "color by Deluxe" are each printed twice in different ways, but this difference has no effect on either grammar or lexis.

CINECITY SCIENCE FICTION FESTIVAL

Feb.13 IT'S OUT OF THIS WORLD!!! FORBIDDEN PLANET — CINEMASCOPE • COLOR

ADDED FOR LAFFS!

Feb.20 INVASION OF THE BODY SNATCHERS — SUPERSCOPE

Feb.27 H. G. WELLS' THE TIME MACHINE IN METROCOLOR

March 6 H.G. WELLS' THE WAR OF THE WORLDS TECHNICOLOR

March 13 PLANET OF THE APES — COLOR by DeLuxe — PANAVISION

March 20 JOURNEY TO THE CENTER OF THE C...

THE ASTOUNDING 15 PART SERIAL "THE LOST PLANET"

every friday at 11.45pm • all seats $2.00

EXERCISES:

1. The typeface of "Cinecity Science Fiction Festival" was probably selected because it would be recognized by many readers. In what situation is it familiar? Is this situation important in this advertisement?

2. Rewrite the advertisement in a paragraph of conventional English prose, and discuss the features you were forced to leave out.

PHONOLOGY

A rather effective radio commercial begins with the following dialogue between host and guest:

Guest: Say this is some party.

Host: Well I'm glad you're enjoying yourself . . . I figure if you're going to have a Golden, why not invite your friends to join you.

Guest: A gold-in? I didn't know you were active in the uh hippie movement.

Our transcription of this originally spoken text into conventional English orthography has involved the loss of many features important to its meaning. The following phonemic transcription allows us to represent more phonological features on paper:

/sey d̃is iz səm partiy/

/wel aym glæd yuw enĵoy+n yurself/

/ay figer iv yur gɔnə hæv ə gowlden way nat invayt

čer frenz tə ĵoyn yə/

/ah gowldin ay didənt now yuw wər æktiv in

d̃iy ə hipiy muwvment/

Such a transcript lets the reader trained in phonetics know many features of the way the passage sounded when spoken. The choice of /gɔnə/ ("gonna") and /figər/ ("figger") mark the text as somewhat informal, and the choices /partiy/ rather than the British (and Boston!) r-less /phatiy/, and /nat/ rather than /nɔt/ suggests that it is spoken in a North American rather than British geographical dialect.

Even this phonemic transcription does not account for all the features of spoken language. Such a transcription notes only the contrasting sounds (segmental phonemes) which can be joined together to make up different words. It does not convey other phonemic features, such as stress, and the changes in pitch constituting intonation contours (suprasegmental phonemes), which are also important in determining the actual meaning of the dialogue.

Take the sentence "I'm glad you're enjoying yourself". Say it aloud a number of times, emphasizing first "I'm", then "glad", then "you're" and finally "enjoying". These changes in stress yield four different meanings. Emphasizing "you're", for example, gives a slightly ironic effect, since it suggests that the speaker is certainly *not* enjoying himself. If the intonation contour of the last four words, "you're enjoying yourself", ends with a rise in pitch, the statement becomes a question. Other features of the way the sentence is spoken — the speed of delivery, the number of hesitations in delivery — also contribute to its meaning.

Spoken language obviously differs considerably from written language. Although we are not able to deal with spoken language directly at the phonological level in a written text, such as the text of this book, we are nevertheless able to discuss its nature and importance. Full descriptions of spoken language at the levels of grammar and lexis can be made.

EXERCISE:
Even without a technical knowledge of phonemics, it is possible and useful to write many of the features of spoken speech. Make a tape recording of a short section of speech, preferably "live" and spontaneous. Play this back in short stretches, listening to each bit until you are totally familiar with it. Write down *everything* you can hear — repeated words, pauses, "fillers" ("er" and "uh" are used to represent quite a wide range of sounds).

GRAMMAR

Anyone who can speak a language has a working command of its grammar; he can perform according to the rules, even though he may not be able to describe them. All of us are familiar with the basic grammatical patterns of English: place the subject after the verb to ask a question, "How tall are you?"; place it before the verb to make a statement, "I'm six feet seven inches tall."; omit the subject to give a command, "Pay at the cashier's desk."

The rules of grammar are not, of course, as simple as these three examples suggest. The pattern of verb before subject, for instance, does not invariably indicate a question. "Will you be home by six" can, depending upon the way in which it is spoken, range in meaning from a question to a command.

Many people who might have difficulty in describing the patterns of English are able to use both the simple patterns of the three examples above and the more complex ones which give rise to the multiple meanings of "Will you be home by six". The term "grammar" designates both the total system of rules to which a language user conforms, and the system of rules which a particular grammarian may have written. The "grammar" of English has been described in many ways. Two modern attempts are Transformational Grammar and Scale-and-Category Grammar.

Within the Scale-and-Category model used in this book, the following concepts are useful for describing varieties of English: the units of English grammar; the rank scale in which they are ordered; the structure of the unit "sentence"; the structure of the unit "clause", and the distinction between major and minor clauses; the structure of the unit "group"; the structure of the unit "word"; morphemes; rankshift; and the scale of delicacy. The concept "nominal group", for example, will allow you to discuss precisely a phrase such as "Combination quicklag and 1, 2 or 3 pole 'E2' Frame Breaker Panelboards", which is an example of modern technical language.

UNITS

Scale-and-Category grammar describes English in terms of five units:

sentence

clause

group

word

morpheme

These units are ranked in terms of their inclusiveness.
Every unit is made up of one or more occurrences of the unit immediately below it, except for the morpheme, which is the smallest unit.

Clauses (one or more) make up sentences:

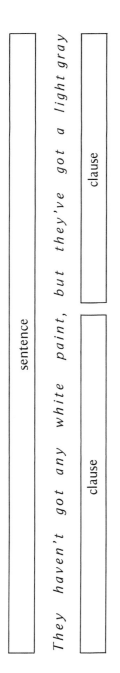

Groups (one or more) make up clauses:

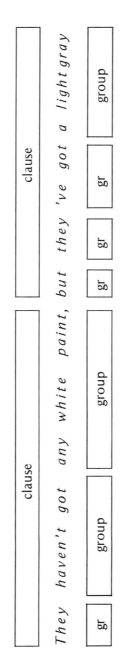

Words (one or more) make up groups:

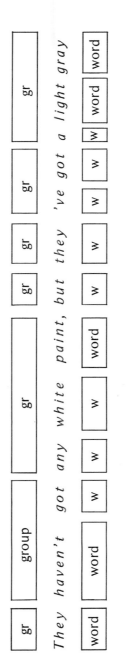

Morphemes (one or more) make up words:

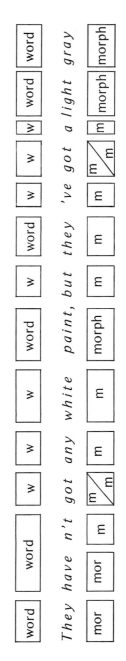

13

The unit is at the top of the rank scale does not itself make up a larger unit. This, in fact, is its definition: A sentence is a unit of grammar which is not a part of a larger grammatical unit. All of the following are sentences:

(1) Damn!

(2) *The Sound and the Fury*

(3) I read *The Sound and the Fury*.

(4) Mow the lawn, if you have the time.

(5) They haven't got any white paint, but they've got a light gray.

This definition accounts for units not traditionally thought of as sentences, such as example 2, found on the cover of William Faulkner's novel. The same words *The Sound and the Fury* form only a part of the sentence in example 3.

Distinction between Graphological and Grammatical Sentences

Grammar describes grammatical patterns only; graphology describes only graphological patterns. The graphological convention that a sentence begins with a capital letter and ends with a period tells us that the following quotation from G.M. Trevelyan's *A Shortened History of England* consists of two sentences:

In these appeals to individual generosity the two sides were on equal terms, and that was how the war was begun. But the Roundheads had more staying power because they could do what the King could not—negotiate loans in the City, and place regular taxes on the trade of England and on its richest districts.

These are two *graphological* sentences.

The same quotation, when examined in terms of its grammatical patterning is seen to be one sentence consisting of an E^t and an E^+:

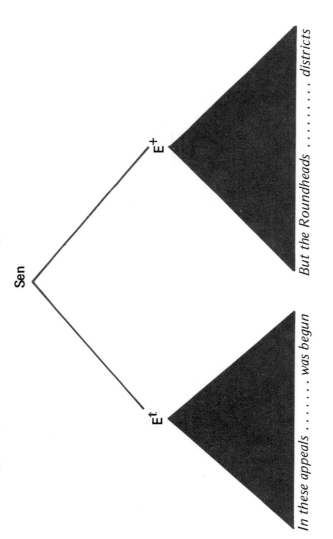

In these appeals . . . . was begun

But the Roundheads . . . . districts

In the above example, two *graphological* sentences constitute one *grammatical* sentence. In another quotation by the same author, the converse is also true. The single *graphological* sentence, "The history of civilized man in our country is very old; it begins long before the reign of Alfred", consists of two *grammatical* sentences:

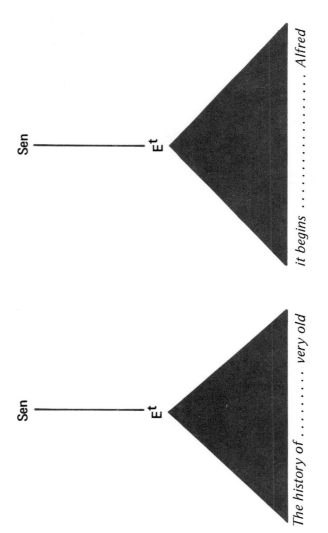

The history of . . . . very old

it begins . . . . Alfred

The ability to recognize the degree to which grammatical and graphological sentences coincide helps greatly in describing the relative formality or informality of a text.

THE STRUCTURE OF THE UNITS

Structure accounts for the patterning of elements within a given unit.

I SENTENCE STRUCTURE

There are two elements of sentence structure: Typical elements (Et) and additioned elements (E+). "Sen" in a diagram indicates a sentence, and Et and E+ indicate its constituent elements. The words making up the elements are written below a triangle.

(1) The cat died.

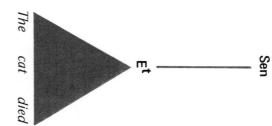

TYPICAL ELEMENTS (Et). Typical elements can, by themselves, constitute a sentence.

(1) The cat died.

ADDITIONED ELEMENTS (E+). Additioned elements cannot by themselves constitute a sentence. They require another element to which they are additioned.

(1) The cat died, but we got a new one.

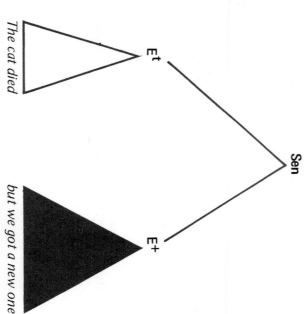

(2) Mow the lawn and then trim the hedge.

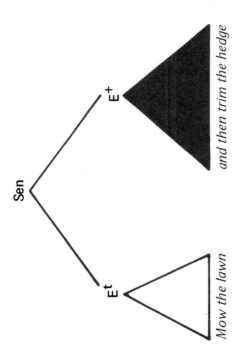

Sen

E^t E$^+$

Mow the lawn *and then trim the hedge*

"If" clauses and similar constructions are not additioned, but are depended. They form a part of an E^t or an E$^+$.

(1) Mow the lawn, if you have the time.

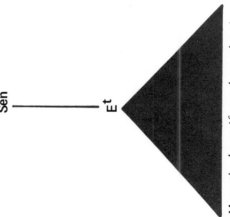

Sen

E^t

Mow the lawn if you have the time

EXERCISE:

Diagram the following sentences, which have a structure of E^t or E^t E$^+$:

1. Go to Beckers and get another quart of milk.

2. Back in ten minutes.

3. The one sitting on the left is the Prime Minister.

4. When the bough breaks, the cradle will fall.

5. 3570 Bloor St.

6. If you insist I'll come, but I'd rather not.

II CLAUSE STRUCTURE

There are five elements of clause structure: predicator (P), subject (S), complement (C), zed (Z), and adjunct (A).

PREDICATOR (P): The predicator is the major element of clause structure, in that all others are determined by their relationship to the predicator. The predicator includes all words in the verbal group.

(1) He may arrive next Tuesday.

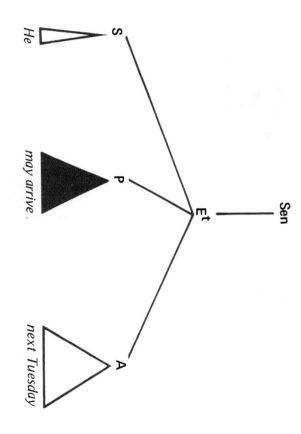

(2) It might have been sent by mail.

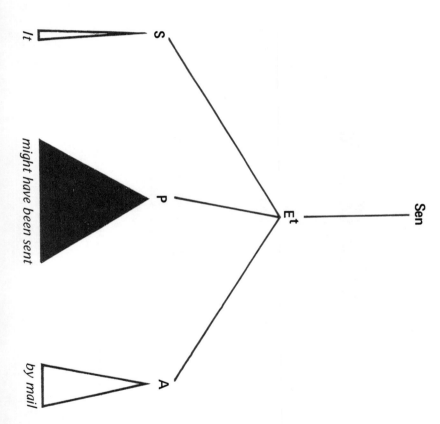

(3) They certainly would have been considered for the position.

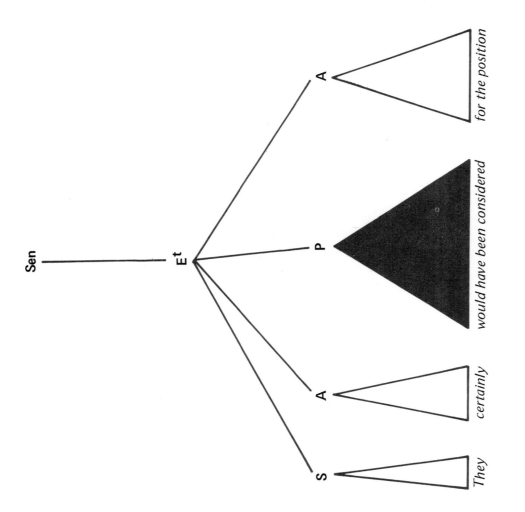

EXERCISE:
Diagram the following sentences, which have a clause structure of subject and predicator:

1. It ought to work.

2. The phone has been disconnected.

3. The file may have been misplaced.

4. Almost all of the applicants for the position have been interviewed.

5. We deliver.

6. No reasonable offer will be refused.

SUBJECT (S): The subject is the element which usually comes immediately before, or interrupts, the predicator.

(1)   In this light it looks a lot better.

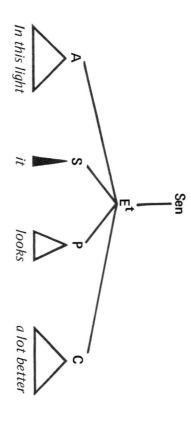

(2)   Could you give me my change in quarters, please?

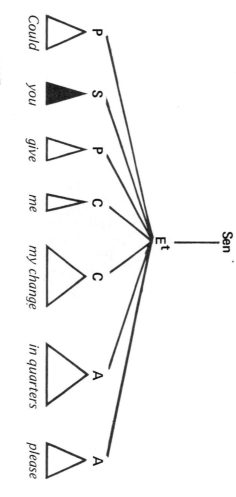

EXERCISE:

Diagram the following sentences, which have a clause structure of subject and predicator; or one of predicator, subject, and predicator:

1.   Would the one on the outside do?

2.   You don't say.

3.   A 3-inch number twelve woodscrew ought to fit.

4.   Should other alternatives have been considered?

5.   Trespassers will be prosecuted.

6.   Last year's report on mining prospects in northern Ontario is being updated.

COMPLEMENT (C): The complement usually follows the predicator.

(1) I bashed the car in yesterday.

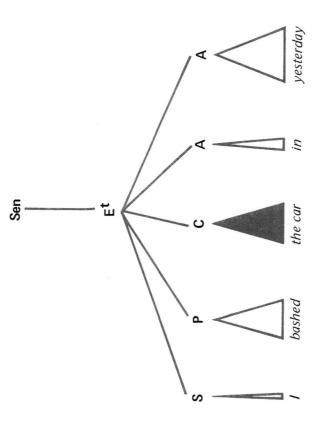

(2) She's the best secretary we've ever had.

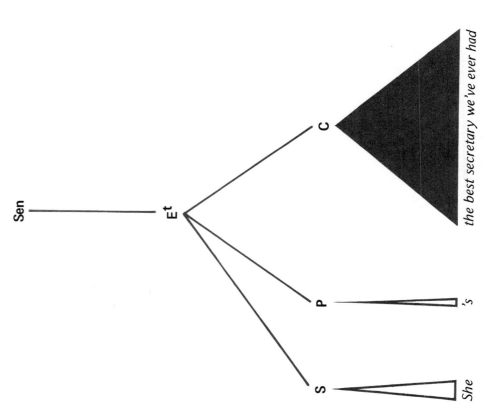

It is possible to have more than one complement in the same clause. A **DATIVE COMPLEMENT** (Cd) frequently occurs with an **OBJECTIVE COMPLEMENT** (Co). When the dative complement does *not* have a "to" or "for", it comes first.

(1)   I sent Harry a new tie.

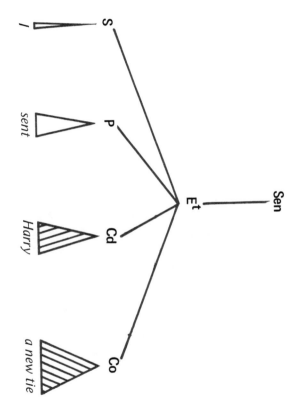

When the dative complement has a "to" or "for" it follows the objective complement.

(1)   I made a hallowe'en costume for my sister.

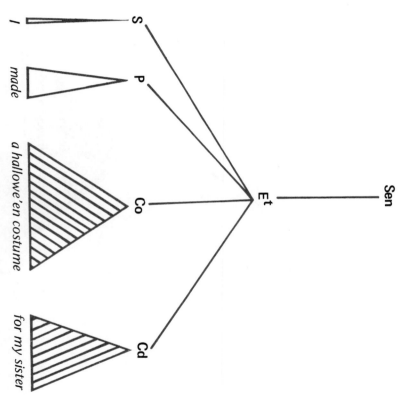

Both objective and dative complements complement the *predicator*. A
COPULAR COMPLEMENT (Cc) complements the *subject*.

(1)   This ice cream tastes terrible.

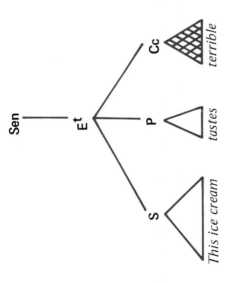

(2)   The new stainless steel knives are more effective.

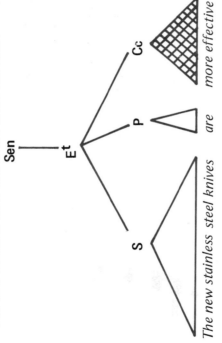

(3)   She returned, broken-hearted.

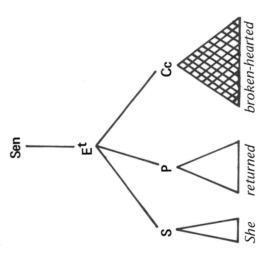

The relationship between subject and copular complement is clearly seen in the following phrases:

(1)   The terrible ice cream.

(2)   The more effective new stainless steel knives.

(3)   The broken-hearted woman.

EXERCISE:

Diagram the following sentences which have a clause structure of subject, predicator, complement, but not necessarily in that order:

1.   What do you mean?

2.   The finance company repossessed my TV.

3.   I like running a general store.

4.   I'll send him a telegram.

5.   These bananas are rotten.

6.   We buy and sell used musical instruments.

ZED (Z): Zed elements occur without overt relationship to a predicator. They can occur in a clause without a predicator (a minor clause).

(1) Nuts!

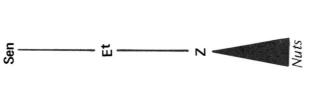

The Zed may be alone, or it may appear with other elements of clause structure.

(2) Two dollars worth of gas, please.

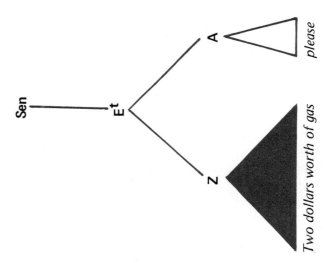

Zed elements also occur in clauses with predicators (major clauses) to which, however, they are not overtly related:

(3)   John, could you come here a minute?

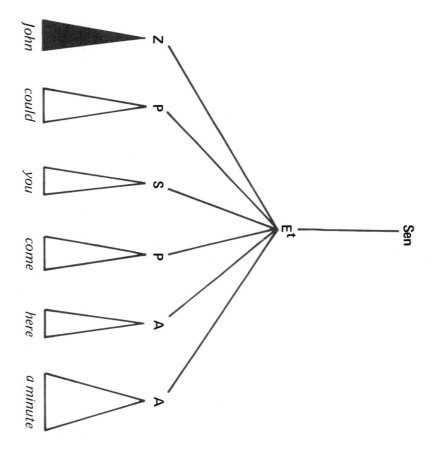

EXERCISE:

Diagram the following sentences, each of which has a Zed element as part of its clause structure:

1.   My fellow Canadians, we must unite.

2.   Danger!

3.   Pictorial Display Studio

4.   Weekly Summary of Shipments, Inventories and Purchases

5.   The Barbizon School of Modelling

6.   What does this mean, Albert?

ADJUNCT (A): Adjunct denotes any clause element other than S, P, C, or Zed. Adjuncts can be found at the beginning, middle or end of a clause.

(1) I tried to call you, but the line was busy.

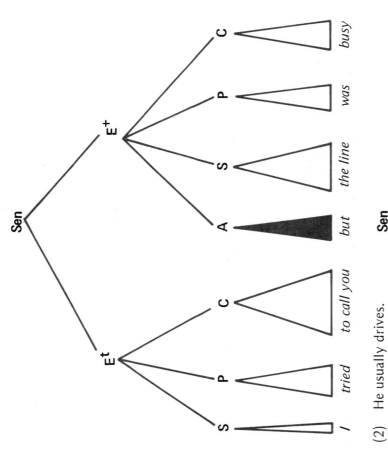

(2) He usually drives.

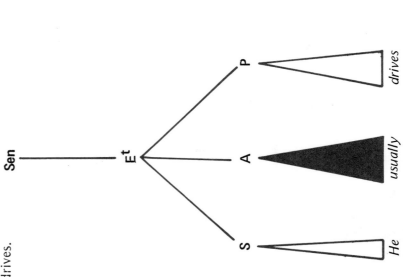

(3) Dylan Thomas, born Oct. 22, 1914, in Swansea, Wales, died in New York City on Nov. 9, 1953.

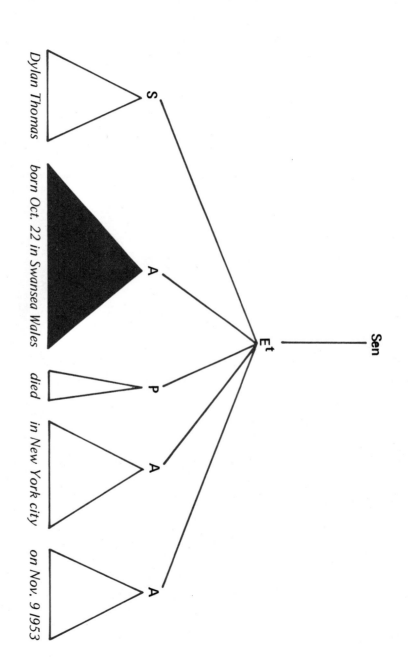

(4) He covered it with wallboard.

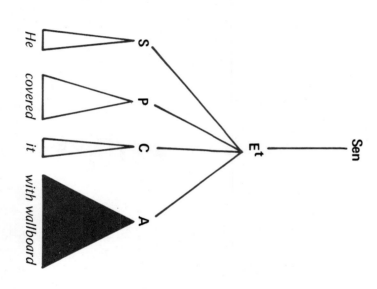

(5) He painted it white, which was a great improvement.

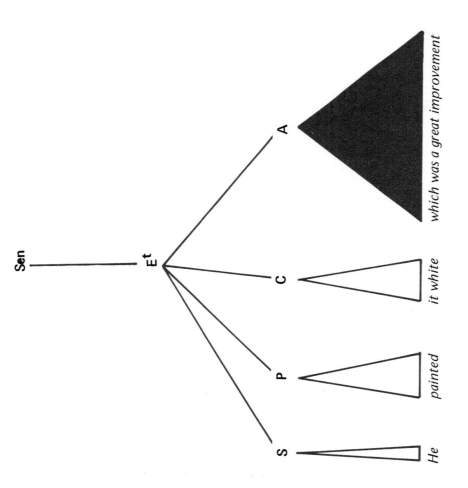

EXERCISE:
Diagram the following sentences, each of which has one or more adjuncts as part of its clause structure:

1. She is always invited.

2. On the other hand, he might be right.

3. She's joined, and therefore she must pay her dues.

4. Eventually you'll understand.

5. In England they drive on the left.

6. *Vanity Fair*, a nineteenth-century novel, is currently being shown on television.

III GROUP STRUCTURE

NOMINAL GROUP STRUCTURE. There are three elements in the structure of a nominal group: **MODIFIER** (M), **HEAD** (H), and **QUALIFIER** (Q).

HEAD (H): The nominal head is easily recognized, because it is the element which must be present.

(1) Houses are expensive in Toronto.

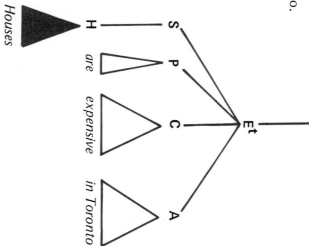

MODIFIER (M): Any element which occurs before the head is a modifier.

(2) Good-sized houses . . . .

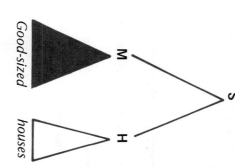

QUALIFIER (Q): Any element following the head is a qualifier.

(3) Good-sized houses in a middle-class neighbourhood . . . . .

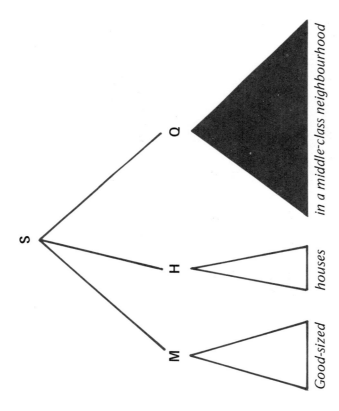

Good-sized   houses   in a middle-class neighbourhood

EXERCISE:

Diagram the following subjects, which have a nominal group structure of a head with possible modifiers or qualifiers. Omit the "Sen" for sentence and "Et" for element. Begin with "S" for subject:

1. One-eyed Jacks . . . . .

2. Politicians without principles . . . . . .

3. The first one who crosses the finish line . . . . .

4. The following additional examples . . . . . .

5. The quadrantal deviation due to unsymmetrical iron . . . . . .

6. Kitchen remodelling . . . . . .

VERBAL GROUP STRUCTURE. There are two possible elements in the structure of a verbal group: **AUXILIARY** (X) and **HEAD** (H). The head, if present, will always be the last element.

(1)   . . . might have been pushed . . . .

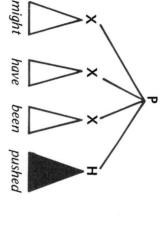

might   have   been   pushed

(2)   . . . will be considered . . . .

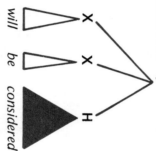

will   be   considered

(3)   . . . has applied . . . .

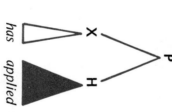

has   applied

(4)   Stop!

A verbal group may have only a head.

Stop

Or it may have one (or more) auxiliary elements, and no head, as in the second clause of the sentence "I wasn't considered for the job, and with my experience in the company, I ought to have been."

(5) . . . ought to have been . . . .

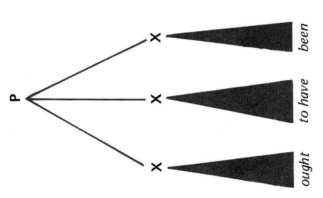

EXERCISE:
Diagram the following verbal groups, omitting "Sen", and "Et", and beginning with "p":

1. . . . might have been (in "John was popular, and Roger might have been if he'd cared".)

2. . . . was being processed . . . .

3. . . . ought to have been applied . . . .

4. . . . jumps . . . .

5. . . . have to be considered . . . .

6. . . . will go . . . .

PREPOSITIONAL GROUP STRUCTURE. There are two basic elements in the structure of a prepositional group: **PREPOSITION** (p) and **COMPLETIVE** (c). Note that these are printed in lower case to distinguish them from predicator (P) and complement (C).

PREPOSITION (p): The preposition is always the first element of the group.

(1) . . . by ship . . . .

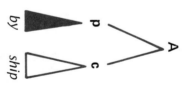

        by   ship

(2) . . . under the bridge . . . .

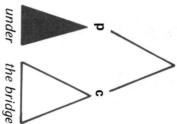

    under   the bridge

(3) . . . after the attack . . . .

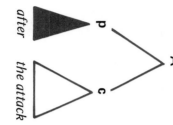

    after   the attack

COMPLETIVE (c): The completive, like the preposition, can sometimes be a single word.

(1) . . . by ship . . . . .

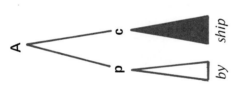

A
p   c

by   *ship*

(2) . . . up there . . . . .

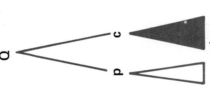

Q
p   c

up   *there*

Usually, however, the completive consists of a larger unit. The preposition "until", for example, can take as its completive a word.

(3) . . . until ten . . . . .

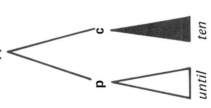

A
p   c

until   *ten*

It can also take a group as completive.

(4) . . . until the last moment . . . . .

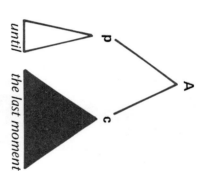

until   the last moment

It can also take a clause as completive.

(5) . . . until the cows come home . . . .

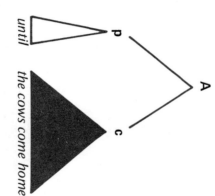

until   the cows come home

EXERCISE:

Diagram the following sentences, each of which contains at least one prepositional group as an adjunct element in its clause structure:

1. The river babbled with a delightful sound.

2. Proceed with caution!

3. Be home before midnight.

4. Sweet Thames, run softly, till I end my song.

5. *Across the River and into the Trees*

6. We maintain your lighting system at peak efficiency.

IV   WORD STRUCTURE

There are two elements of word structure: a **BASE MORPHEME** (B) which must be present, and one or more **AFFIX MORPHEMES** (A), which are optional. Affix morphemes, if present, may occur at the beginning, middle, or end of a word, or at all of these positions.

BASE (B): A word may consist of a base only.

(1) . . . form . . . .

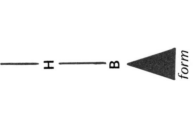

form

If an affix occurs at the beginning, it is called an **AFFIX PREFIX** (Ap)

(2) . . . reform . . . .

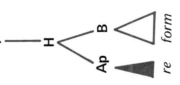

re   form

If it occurs at the end it is called **AFFIX SUFFIX** (As)

(3) . . . reformed . . . . .

re   form   ed

At times a change in structure occurs in the middle of a word. This change is called **AFFIX INFIX** (Ai). "Goose" is a word which changes its form in this way. By convention the term Ai is written after the base of the word undergoing change.

(4) . . . geese . . . .

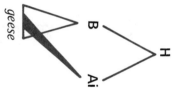

Not all base morphemes can constitute a word without an affix. There is a common base in the words introject, reject, and injection, which is never found by itself. Such a base is called **BASE BOUND** (Bb).

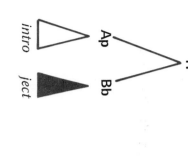

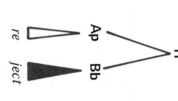

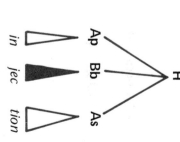

EXERCISE:

Diagram the *italicized* words beginning at the element of clause structure in which the word is found:

1. *Promote* all our products.

2. The *promotion* went well.

3. His *demotion* upset him.

4. She *ran* fast.

5. I *run* fast.

6. There it *goes*.

V STRUCTURE AND THE MORPHEME

— The morpheme plays a part in the structure of words (see previous page), but there is no constituent element playing a part in it. Therefore the morpheme cannot be said to have structure.

VI RANKSHIFT AND FLOW DIAGRAMS

Two concepts are important for understanding rankshift: the units which constitute stretches of language, and the structure of the elements which make up the units.

In the following flow diagrams, units are written out, and their structures are represented by symbols. Each unit can be seen to be related to two structures: that of the unit on the line above, and its own structure, which is printed on the line below. The sentence "They haven't got any white paint, but they've got a light gray" has no rankshifted units, and therefore in *flow diagram A* each line of structural elements is different.

Notice that the elements of structure of any given unit consist of the units immediately below on the rank scale. The second line contains both possible elements of sentence structure (E^t and E^+), the fourth contains four of the five elements of clause structure (S P C A Z), the sixth contains three of the elements of group structure (M H Q X H p c), and the eighth contains both of the elements of word structure (A and B).

The sentence "They haven't got any white paint because they forgot the order" contains a rankshifted clause. This is clearly seen in *flow diagram B*. The second line contains only elements of sentence structure, and the fourth contains only elements of clause structure. The sixth line, however, contains two kinds of elements: the first six (H X H M M H) are elements of group structure, but the last four (A S P C) are elements of clause structure. The lines above these four (A S P C) converge upon "because they forgot the order", which is therefore a clause unit.

This occurrence of a unit clause as an element of structure within a clause is an example of rankshift.

FLOW DIAGRAM A

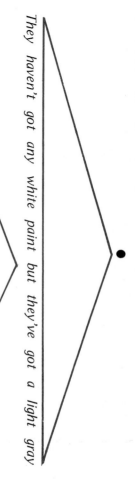

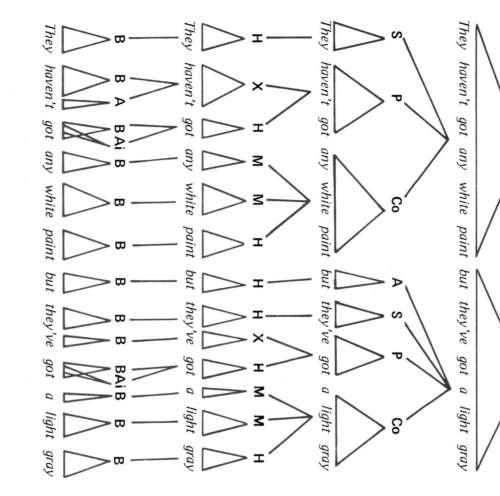

1. SENTENCE (unit)

They haven't got any white paint but they've got a light gray

2. SENTENCE ELEMENTS (structure)

E^t E^+

3. CLAUSES

They haven't got any white paint but they've got a light gray

4. CLAUSE ELEMENTS (structure)

S   P   Co   A   S   P   Co

5. GROUPS (units)

They haven't got any white paint but they've got a light gray

6. GROUP ELEMENTS (structure)

H   X   H   M   M   H   H   X   H   M   M   H

7. WORDS (units)

They haven't got any white paint but they've got a light gray

8. WORD ELEMENTS (structure)

B   B   A   BAi   B   B   B   B   B   BAi   B   B

9. MORPHEMES (units)

They haven't got any white paint but they've got a light gray

● No grammatical pattern has been found for which this unit can be the direct exponent of an element of structure.

FLOW DIAGRAM B

1. SENTENCE (unit)

2. SENTENCE ELEMENTS (structure)

3. CLAUSE (unit)

4. CLAUSE ELEMENTS (structure)

5. GROUPS and CLAUSE (units)

6. GROUP ELEMENTS and CLAUSE ELEMENTS (structure)

7. WORDS and GROUPS (units)

8. WORD ELEMENTS and GROUP ELEMENTS (structure)

9. MORPHEMES and WORDS (units)

10. WORD ELEMENTS (structure)

11. MORPHEMES (units)

41

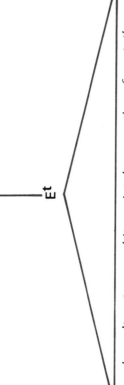

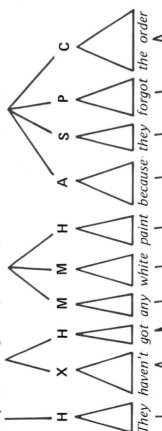
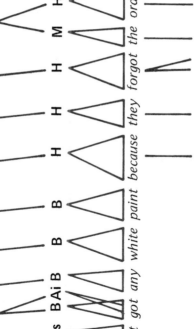
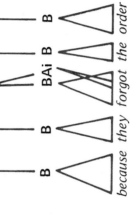

They haven't got any white paint because they forgot the order

E^t

They haven't got any white paint because they forgot the order.

S   P   C   A

They haven't got any white paint because they forgot the order

H   X   H   M   M   H   A   S   P   C

They haven't got any white paint because they forgot the order

B   B   As   BAi   B   B   B   H   H   H   H   M   H

They have n't got any white paint because they forgot the order

B   B   BAi   B   B   BAi   B   B

because they forgot the order

42

The unit clause can also fulfill a structural role in smaller units. In "They didn't have the paint which I wanted", the clause "which I wanted" makes up the structural element Q within the unit group.

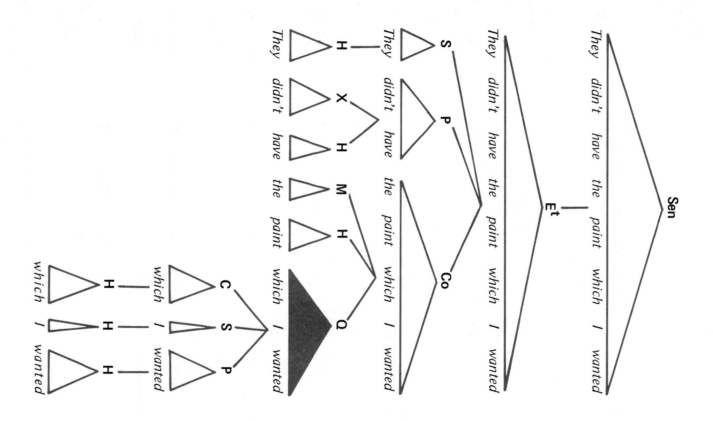

EXERCISE:

If a given unit has any of its elements of structure realized by a unit of the same or higher rank, rankshift has occurred. For each of the following three diagrams:

(1) State the unit which is rankshifted, the structural element which it makes up, and

(2) Specify whether the rankshifted unit is operating in the structure of a unit of the same or lower rank.

Sample: He picked the forget-me-not.

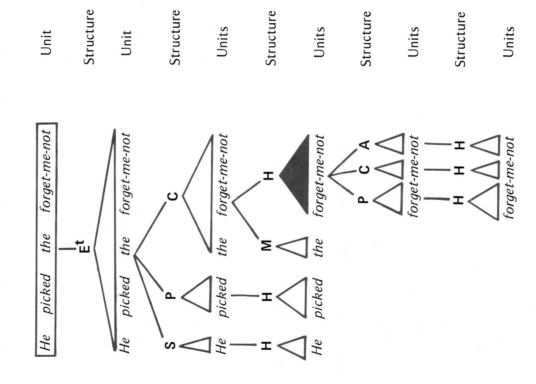

Sample Answer: "(1) The unit which is rankshifted is the clause 'forget-me-not' which makes up the head element of structure of the group 'the forget-me-not'. (2) The rankshifted clause is operating in a unit of lower rank (group)."

43

44

(1)   The two key sentences were: "I hated him. I bought the gun and I used it."

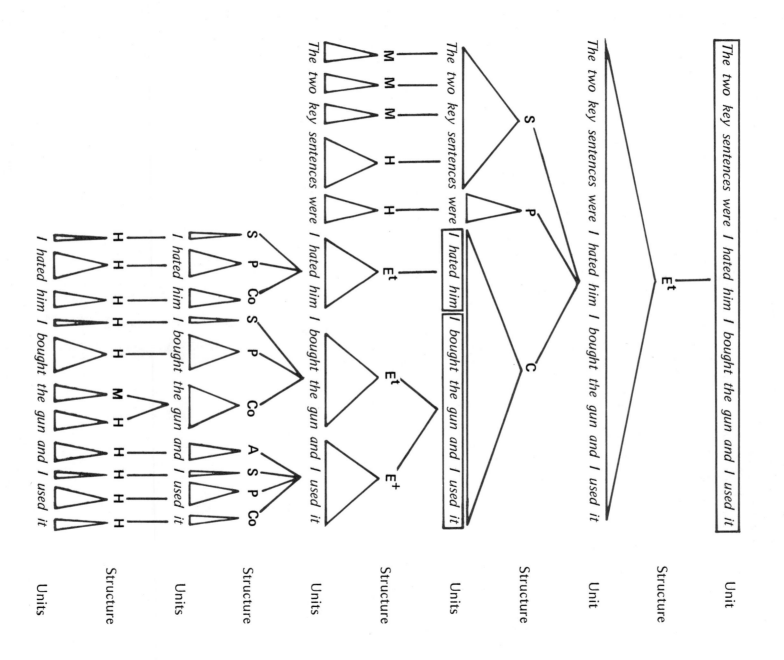

(2) If you try you can do it.

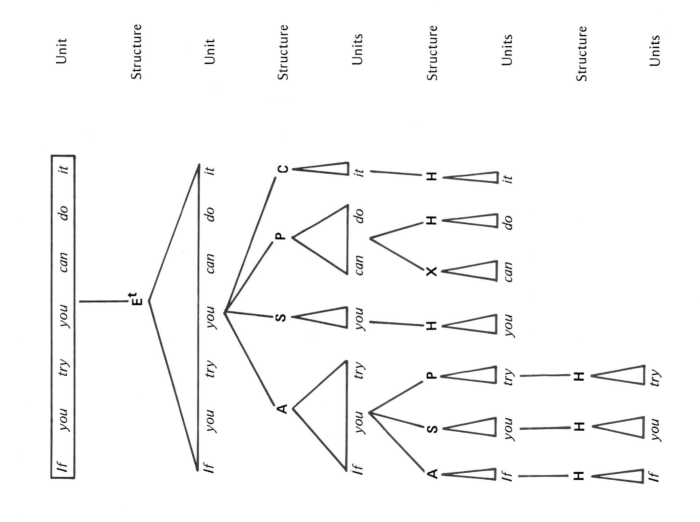

45

(3)   The man she loved loved another woman.

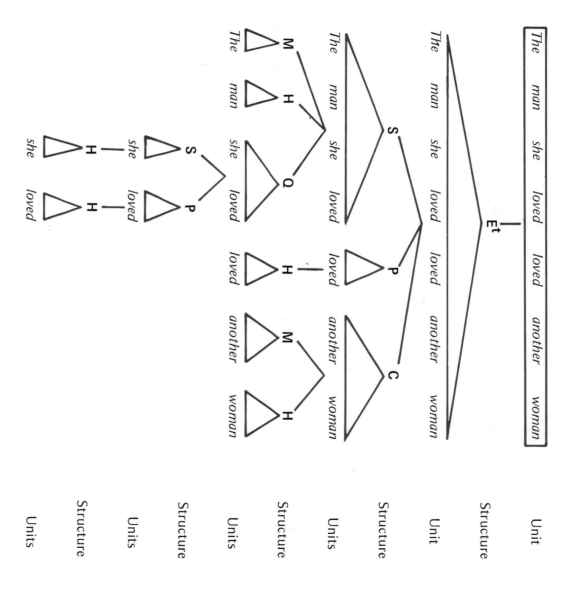

| The | man | she | loved | loved | another | woman | Unit |

Structure

| The | man | she | loved | loved | another | woman | Unit |

S   E^t   Structure

Units

Structure

Units

Structure

Units

Structure

Units

EXERCISE:

Diagram the following sentences, each of which contains a rankshifted unit.
Omit word structure (morphemes) from your diagram.

1. I saw the man steal the watch.

2. The fish I caught tastes good.

3. I'll come when I can.

FLOW DIAGRAMS OF STRUCTURE

Normally flow diagrams do not include the grammatical unit making up each element; instead, the diagram goes directly to the structure of that unit. Only at the final stage of description does the diagram introduce the stretch of language which constitutes the structural element immediately above it.

The sentence "They haven't got any white paint, but they've got a light gray" would, therefore, be diagrammed:

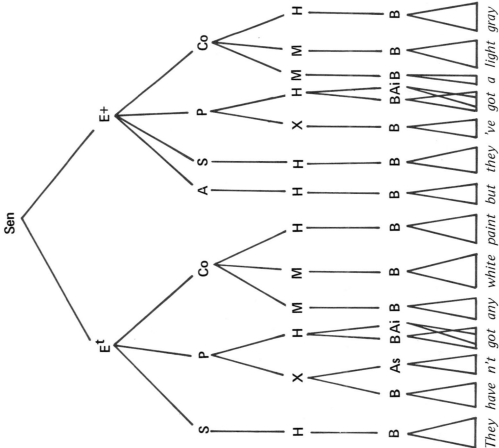

The choice of the final point at which the diagram stops describing structure and introduces the grammatical units operating in structure depends on the purpose of the analysis. In describing children's speech a very simple diagram might suffice to show that the normal pattern is one of long sentences consisting of many linked elements. For example: "Mommy came home and gave me a candy and I saw Roger and I said hello and he said . . . (et cetera)".

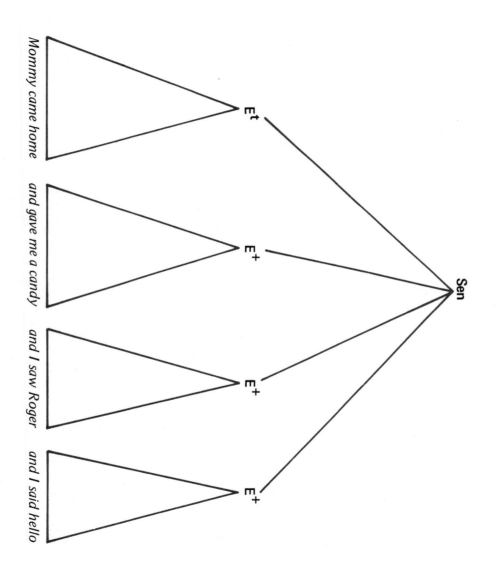

The opening two sentences of F. Scott Fitzgerald's novel *Tender is the Night* do not yield much information when analysed only in terms of sentence elements.

(1) On the pleasant shore of the French Riviera, about halfway between Marseilles and the Italian border, stands a large, proud, rose-colored hotel.

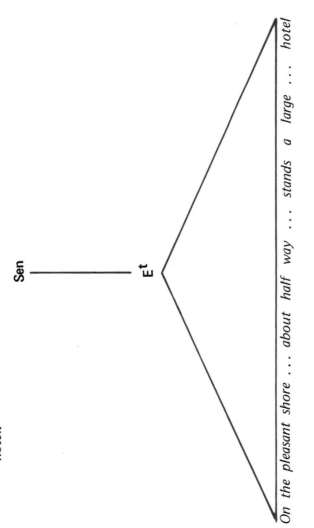

Sen

Eᵗ

On the pleasant shore ... about half way ... stands a large ... hotel

(2) Deferential palms cool its flushed façade, and before it stretches a short dazzling beach.

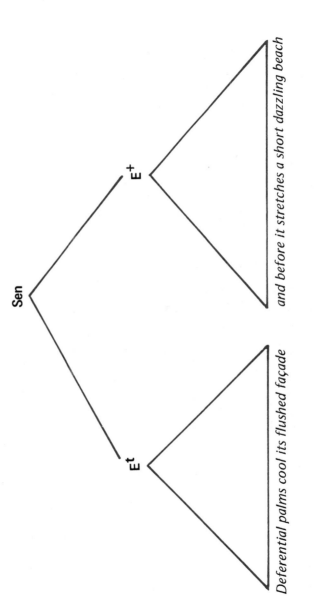

Sen

Eᵗ   E⁺

Deferential palms cool its flushed façade

and before it stretches a short dazzling beach

An analysis of the elements of clause structure, however, reveals a change from the normal order of SPCA.

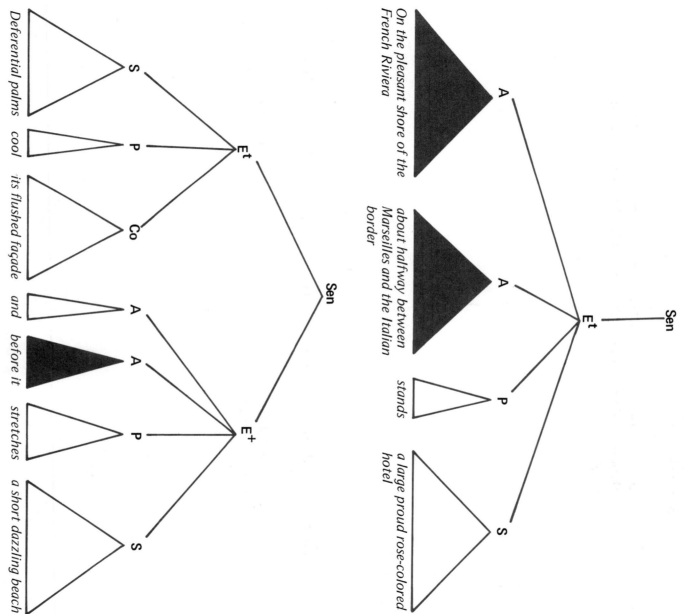

On the pleasant shore of the French Riviera $[A]$ about halfway between Marseilles and the Italian border $[A]$ stands $[P]$ a large proud rose-colored hotel $[S]$ $[E^t]$ $[Sen]$

Deferential palms $[S]$ cool $[P]$ its flushed façade $[Co]$ $[E^t]$ and before it $[A]$ $[A]$ stretches $[P]$ a short dazzling beach $[S]$ $[E^+]$ $[Sen]$

In the first and third clauses the subject *follows* the predicator, and the initial element of clause structure, a key position, is filled by adjuncts describing place: "On the pleasant shore of the French Riviera" and "before it". It would be impossible to show how "place" is made the theme of the clause without taking the diagram at least as far as clause structure.

51

Although the two sentences describe physical setting, they do so in metaphoric language. The inclusion of human characteristics can be seen in the group structures "a large, proud, rose-colored hotel" and "its flushed façade".

(1) . . . a large, proud, rose-colored hotel . . . .

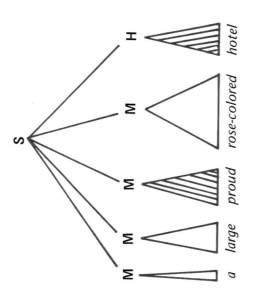

(2) . . . its flushed façade . . . .

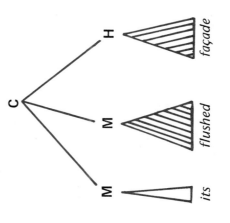

In each case the head of the group is an inanimate object, but one of the modifiers is normally an attribute of a human. This relationship is not entirely explained at the level of grammar; these modifiers and the heads are lexical items (see next section) as well as grammatical units.

SCALE OF DELICACY. In describing patterns, it is important to be able to show both likeness and difference. In the group "the heavy oak table", for instance, the likeness of the modifiers "the", "heavy", and "oak" is shown by their common designation "M".

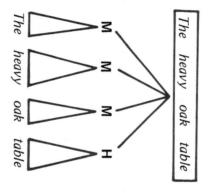

While they have in common their occurrence before the head of the group, the three modifiers are not similar in every respect. "Oak" is a nominal modifier, and as such will always occupy the position immediately before the head. ("The oak heavy table" is not an acceptable alternative.) In a flow diagram of greater delicacy, nominal modifiers are indicated by adding s (for substantive) to the symbol M. "Heavy" is also place-oriented, and will always occur immediately before substantive modifiers. It is an adjective, and is indicated in diagrams by adding e (for epithet). "The" will always occur before adjectives are introduced. Its initial place in structure is indicated by the symbol d (for deictic). At secondary delicacy the group would therefore read:

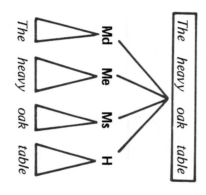

Statements of greater delicacy can continue to be made as long as criteria for making distinctions among similar things can be found.

SYSTEM AND CLASS

Language is sequential. At certain points in the sequence the speaker must select from a fixed number of grammatical options. In the process of speaking a nominal group, for example, he must at some point utter the head of that group. The lexical nature of that head is infinite (corn, courage, cow, Roger, green, Mother's, et cetera), but the grammatical options are fixed.

At primary delicacy there is a three-term system at the head of a nominal group. The speaker must select one of the terms: his choice may be a nominal head (cheese, Roger, you), an adjectival head (green, huge, unacceptable) or a deictic head (father's, both, thirteenth). The number of options constitutes a system; each option is called a term in the system.

The actual units which make up the head can be usefully sorted out by another category in Scale-and-Category grammar: the category "class". All cases of the unit word which can operate at Me in structure, for example, belong to the class "adjective". They are adjectival words.

Class, of course, is not limited to the unit word. Any unit may be described in terms of its possibility of operation in the structure of the unit above it on the rank scale. For example, all cases of the unit group, such as "might have been told", "will be arriving" and "has been con- sidered" belong to the class "verbal group" because they can make up the predicator in a clause. The unit clause may be classified in several ways. Those clauses which can operate directly in the structure of a sentence are of the class "independent clause" ("I saw Mary" or ". . . and Roger thinks so too"). Those clauses which cannot operate directly in sentence structure, but must make up part of the structure of a lower unit (clause, group or word) are of the class "dependent clause" (". . . which I would consider seriously . . ." or ". . . that he even thought about it . . .").

LEXIS

The patterns of grammar are *relatively* fixed. For example, a noun with a number system must be either singular or plural: apple/apples, man/men, wolf/wolves. That is the extent of the number choice. Another example: Consider the statement "I eat". Grammar admits the possibility of its having, or its not having, a complement or an adjunct, or both a complement and an adjunct, or more than one of these. Any choice must, however, be made from the fixed elements of clause structure.

Examples:　　I eat *good food*　(S P C)

I eat *slowly*　(S P A)

I eat *good food slowly*　(S P C A)

I eat　(S P)

The range of grammatical choice is limited.

Lexis is concerned with a different kind of pattern. A purely lexical study ignores the grammatical fact of the predicator-complement relationship and notes simply that "eat" and "food" (or any of the other choices) occur near each other.

The tendency of certain lexical items to occur near each other is called *collocation*. Collocation is described in terms of probability. "Rare", for example, is likely to occur near the two items "medium" and "steak". The collocation of "eat" and "cement", on the other hand, is far less likely. Improbable lexical collocations do occur, however. Poetry characteristically creates a lexical environment in which unexpected collocations make sense, as in Leonard Cohen's lines "*Shelves of staircase people/feed their transistors*".*

Collocating lexical items form *lexical sets* — groups of lexical items that are likely to occur in the presence of one another, such as "wet", "slimy", "slippery", "muddy"; or "teller", "deposit", "withdrawal

*Parasites of Heaven, Leonard Cohen. McClelland & Stewart Ltd.

slip", "counter", or "steeply", "sharply", "altitude", "stabilizer". Such lexical sets are an important factor in generating meaning. The word "bank", for example, will take on a different meaning depending on which lexical set it is found in. The word "bank" is thus a different lexical item in each of these examples: "I deposited fifty dollars in the *bank* today", "I *banked* sharply, as the altimeter read 4,500 feet", and "I slipped on the muddy *bank*". A lexical set is thus a group of lexical items which tend to occur together and mutually generate meaning.

A single word or phrase can be two (or more) lexical items if there are two (or more) lexical sets in which it participates. An example of this is the pun. In the joke "What did the bug say when he hit the windshield?" — "I haven't got the guts to do that again!", the word "guts" is one lexical item in the lexical set "courage", "hero", "danger", and another lexical item in the set "liver", "kidneys", "messy".

"Media Installation"

The lexical analysis of an actual text involves both statistical precision and intuition. (Intuition is used here as an informal term for reliance on our capacity as native speakers to recognize patterns of collocation.) By employing this double process it is possible to discover, without running to a friend or a dictionary, the lexical meaning of "media", which will at first probably baffle most readers of the following text.

The first stage is to circle "media" every time the item occurs, and to underline the two lexical items before it and the two lexical items after it. (The choice of two rather than one, three or four is arbitrary.) The underlined items are then listed in terms of their frequency of occurrence.

MEDIA INSTALLATION
FOR
HORIZONTAL CONOMATIC AND CONOMANUAL

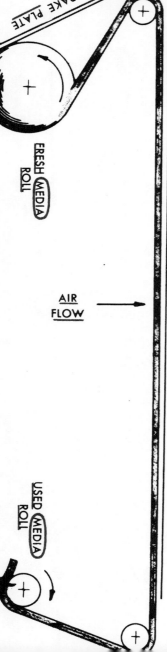

BRAKE PLATE

FRESH MEDIA ROLL

AIR FLOW

USED MEDIA ROLL

A. Horizontal Conomatic (END LOADING)

1. Install small top trunnion in top of core in clean media roll and base trunnion (rectangular shaped) into bottom of core in fresh media roll.

2. Open doors on both ends of filter, remove roll locks from all trunnion tracks.

3. Insert fresh media roll (with trunnions in place) into filter opposite the motor end of filter. Base trunnion must be on bottom and MEDIA MUST FEED FROM CLEAN ROLL SO THAT EXTERIOR OF CLEAN ROLL BECOMES AIR ENTERING SIDE OF FILTER WHEN MEDIA IS UNROLLED IN THE AIRSTREAM. SPECIAL NOTE: On "stacked" (two units high horizontal assemblies) geared trunnion must be ON THE BOTTOM of the upper section and geared trunnion must be ON THE TOP of the lower section.

4. Guide the trunnions into the trunnion track exerting pressure against the brake plate with the media roll.

5. Replace roll lock into upper trunnion track.

6. Insert large lower trunnion into bottom end of empty media core, engaging geared trunnion with drive pin inside core.

7. Insert empty core and trunnions into trunnion tracks in motor end of filter with gear trunnion on the bottom.

8. Mesh gear trunnion and drive sprocket, and replace roll locks into upper and lower trunnion tracks.

9. Feed loose end of clean media roll between idler roller and end of filter.

10. Pull clean media across filter between front and rear grids and between edge seals being careful that media enters both edge seals evenly.

11. Feed end of media around splined metering roller (plain idler roller in Conomanuals).

12. Feed end of media underneath and around empty core and nail (with roofing nails provided) to core at least 2" from end of media. Nails should be about 6" apart.

13. Recheck above steps to be sure all steps have been followed correctly. Filter is now ready to operate.

B. Horizontal Conomatic (FRONT LOADING)

1. Follow all steps above. Only difference is that filter does not have doors and media must be loaded and removed from the air entering side of filter

a. Brake plate must be rotated on its hinges until it points nearly upstream before inserting fresh media roll. After clean media has been installed, allow brake plate to rest against clean media roll.

C. Horizontal Conomanual

1. Insert trunnions into clean media core, LARGE TRUNNIONS ON BOTTOM.

2. Pull out brake plate and install trunnions into trunnion shaft retainers on media holding frame. MEDIA MUST FEED SO THAT EXTERIOR OF CLEAN ROLL BECOMES AIR ENTERING SIDE OF FILTER WHEN MEDIA IS UNROLLED IN THE AIR-STREAM.

3. After installing clean media allow brake plate to rest against clean media roll.

4. Install empty core with large trunnion on bottom into dirty media core holders.

5. Feed media through filter and secure to empty core, following steps Nos. 9 through 13 as outlined above.

TO INSTALL REPLACEMENT MEDIA

A. Remove empty core from unit.

B. Remove trunnions from empty core.

C. Follow steps above for particular type unit involved.

This straightforward assemblage of information shows that the most frequent collocates are "roll", "clean", "install", and "core" (in that order); our intuition tells us immediately that MEDIA is something with a "core", coming in a "roll" with a "core", which you "install".

By looking at the total list of collocates and using one's intuition, it is possible to recognize three lexical sets in which "media" is participating: a "clean" set, an "install" set, and a "mechanism parts" set:

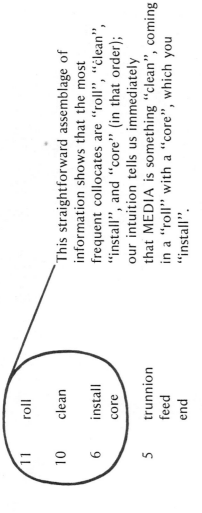

11	roll
10	clean
6	install
	core

5	trunnion
	feed
	end

4	fresh
	filter
	hold

| 3 | plate |
| | empty |

2	insert
	bottom
	side
	unroll
	airstream
	brake
	replace
	inch
	remove
	allow
	rest
	horizontal

1	open
	engage
	idler
	pull
	front
	seal
	careful
	enter
	edge
	spline
	meter
	nail
	door
	load
	large
	shaft
	retain
	dirty
	secure
	frame
	exterior
	air
	use
	flow
	print
	base

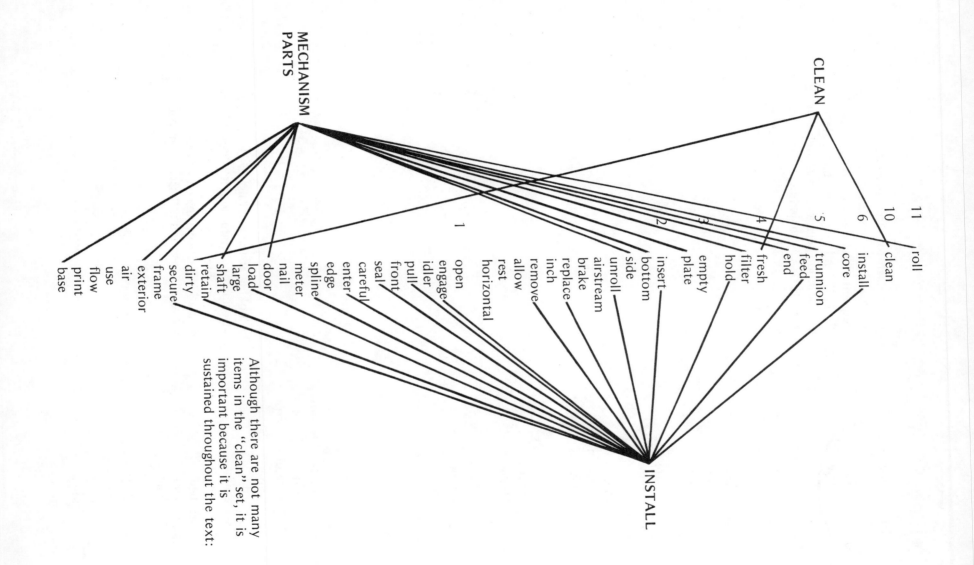

58

MECHANISM
PARTS

CLEAN

INSTALL

11 roll
10 clean
6 install
5 core
4 trunnion
feed
end
3 fresh
filter
hold
2 empty
plate
1 insert
bottom
side
unroll
airstream
brake
replace
inch
remove
allow
rest
horizontal
open
engage
idler
pull
front
seal
careful
enter
edge
spline
meter
nail
door
load
large
shaft
retain
dirty
secure
frame
exterior
air
use
flow
print
base

Although there are not many
items in the "clean" set, it is
important because it is
sustained throughout the text:

MEDIA INSTALLATION
FOR
HORIZONTAL CONOMATIC AND CONOMANUAL

A. Horizontal Conomatic (END LOADING)

1. Install small top trunnion in top of core in clean media roll and base trunnion (rectangular shaped) into bottom of core in fresh media roll.

2. Open doors on both ends of filter, remove roll locks from all trunnion tracks.

3. Insert fresh media roll (with trunnions in place) into filter opposite the motor end of filter. Base trunnion must be on bottom and MEDIA MUST FEED FROM CLEAN ROLL BECOMES AIR ENTERING SIDE OF FILTER WHEN MEDIA IS UNROLLED IN THE AIRSTREAM. SPECIAL NOTE: On "stacked" (two units high horizontal assemblies) geared trunnion must be ON THE BOTTOM of the upper section and geared trunnion must be ON THE TOP of the lower section.

4. Guide ... exerting ... the med...

5. Replace ...

6. Insert la... empty ... with dr...

7. Insert empty core and trunnions into trunnion tracks in motor end of filter with gear trunnion on the bottom.

8. Mesh gear trunnion and drive sprocket, and replace roll locks into upper and lower trunnion tracks.

9. Feed loose end of clean media roll between idler roller and end of filter.

10. Pull clean media across filter between front and rear grids and between edge seals being careful that media enters both edge seals evenly.

11. Feed end of media around splined metering roller (plain idler roller in Conomanuals).

12. Feed end of media underneath and around empty core and nail (with roofing nails provided) to core at least 2" from end of media. Nails should be about 6" apart.

13. Recheck above steps to be sure all steps have been followed correctly. Filter is now ready to operate.

B. Horizontal Conomatic (FRONT LOADING)

1. Follow all steps above. Only difference is that filter does not have doors and media must be loaded and removed from the air entering side of filter

   a. Brake plate must be rotated on its hinges until it points nearly upstream before inserting fresh media roll. After clean media has been installed, allow brake plate to rest against clean media roll.

C. Horizontal Conomanual

1. Insert trunnions into clean media core, LARGE TRUNNIONS ON BOTTOM.

2. Pull out brake plate and install media and trunnions into trunnion shaft retainers on media holding frame. MEDIA MUST FEED SO THAT EXTERIOR OF CLEAN ROLL BECOMES AIR ENTERING SIDE OF FILTER WHEN MEDIA IS UNROLLED IN THE AIRSTREAM.

3. After installing clean media, allow brake plate to rest against clean media roll.

4. Install empty core with large trunnion on bottom into dirty media core holders.

5. Feed media through filter and secure to empty core, following steps Nos. 9 through 13 as outlined above.

TO INSTALL REPLACEMENT MEDIA:

A. Remove empty core from unit.

B. Remove trunnions from empty core.

C. Follow steps above for particular type unit involved.

CLEAN

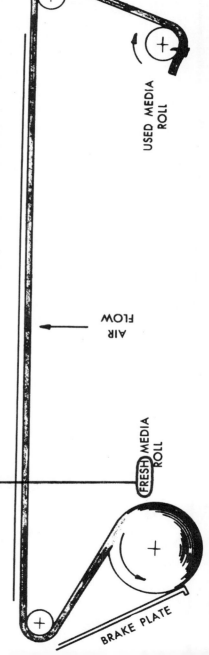

USED MEDIA ROLL

AIR FLOW

FRESH MEDIA ROLL

BRAKE PLATE

PRINTED IN CANADA

FORM B041

60

Understanding lexis through patterns of collocation is the ordinary way you increase your command of the language. It is a familiar experience that a text which seems confused and unclear on a first reading will be much more completely understood after a second reading. Your knowledge of the grammar of English is not likely to have changed at all, but your grasp of the particular lexis at hand will have improved. In dealing with such unusual texts as "Media Installation", it can be useful to make this kind of formal study.

Every occurrence of the lexical item "trunnion" has been circled in the "Media Installation" text, (page 61).

EXERCISES:

1. Underline the two lexical items before, and the two lexical items after, each occurrence of "trunnions". (The choice of the number two is arbitrary. You might choose 1, 2, 3, or any number.)

2. List these in order of frequency.

3. Attempt to find lexical sets among the items listed.

4. Write a short description (based on your lexical analysis in the first three exercises) of what you think a trunnion may be like.

MEDIA INSTALLATION

FOR

HORIZONTAL CONOMATIC AND CONOMANUAL

A. Horizontal Conomatic (END LOADING)

1. Install small top trunnion in top of core in clean media roll and base trunnion (rectangular shaped) into bottom of core in fresh media roll.

2. Open doors on both ends of filter, remove roll locks from all trunnion tracks.

3. Insert fresh media roll (with trunnions in place) into filter opposite the motor end of filter. Base trunnion must be on bottom and MEDIA MUST FEED FROM CLEAN ROLL SO THAT EXTERIOR OF CLEAN ROLL BECOMES AIR ENTERING SIDE OF FILTER WHEN MEDIA IS UNROLLED IN THE AIR-STREAM.
   SPECIAL NOTE: On "stacked" (two units high horizontal assemblies) geared trunnion must be ON THE BOTTOM of the upper section and geared trunnion must be ON THE TOP of the lower section!

4. Guide the trunnions into the trunnion track exerting pressure against the brake plate with the media roll.

5. Replace roll lock into upper trunnion track.

6. Insert large lower trunnion into bottom end of empty media core, engaging geared trunnion with drive pin inside core.

7. Insert empty core and trunnions into trunnion tracks in motor end of filter with gear trunnion on the bottom.

8. Mesh gear trunnion and drive sprocket, and replace roll locks into upper and lower trunnion tracks.

9. Feed loose end of clean media roll between idler roller and end of filter.

10. Pull clean media across filter between front and rear grids and between edge seals being careful that media enters both edge seals evenly.

11. Feed end of media around splined metering roller (plain idler roller in Conomanuals).

12. Feed end of media underneath and around empty core and nail (with roofing nails provided) to core at least 2" from end of media. Nails should be about 6" apart.

13. Recheck above steps to be sure all steps have been followed correctly. Filter is now ready to operate.

B. Horizontal Conomatic (FRONT LOADING)

1. Follow all steps above. Only difference is that filter does not have doors and media must be loaded and removed from the air entering side of filter

   a. Brake plate must be rotated on its hinges until it points nearly upstream before inserting fresh media roll. After clean media has been installed, allow brake plate to rest against clean media roll.

C. Horizontal Conomanual

1. Insert trunnions into clean media core, LARGE TRUNNIONS ON BOTTOM.

2. Pull out brake plate and install media and trunnions into trunnion shaft retainers on media holding frame. MEDIA MUST FEED SO THAT EXTERIOR OF CLEAN ROLL BECOMES AIR ENTERING SIDE OF FILTER WHEN MEDIA IS UNROLLED IN THE AIR-STREAM.

3. After installing clean media, allow brake plate to rest against clean media roll.

4. Install empty core with large trunnion on bottom into dirty media core holders.

5. Feed media through filter and secure to empty core, following steps Nos. 9 through 13 as outlined above.

TO INSTALL REPLACEMENT MEDIA:

A. **Remove empty core from unit.**

B. **Remove trunnions from empty core.**

C. **Follow steps above for particular type unit involved.**

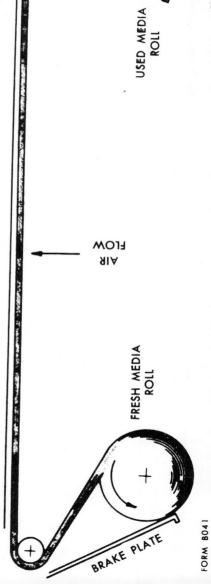

USED MEDIA ROLL

AIR FLOW

FRESH MEDIA ROLL

BRAKE PLATE

FORM B041

In this instance, formal lexical analysis of the collocates of "media" was important because of the unfamiliar way in which "media" was used. Unless a special problem, such as this, exists, it is sufficient to proceed directly to the recognition of lexical sets.

The following text, a letter sent out by the magazine *Intelligence Digest*, contains a number of lexical sets which are separately indicated (pages 63-67).

Persuasion to subscribe is achieved lexically in a complex way. Set (1) creates anxiety, sets (2) and (3) imply status, and sets (4) and (5) offer reassurance.

The writer of the letter was probably not familiar with lexical theory. It is unlikely that he sat down with five lexical sets and wrote a letter around them. The discovery that the sets are there, however, shows one way in which persuasive writing achieves its effect.

Intelligence Digest

AND WEEKLY REVIEW

Now <u>you</u> can receive the best top-level inside <u>information</u> in the world.

Cheltenham, England.

Dear Sir,

What does 1971 hold in store?

We believe that 1971 will be one of the most important years in history.

Each day brings news of some fresh crisis – economic difficulties in Britain and the U.S., new violence in the Arab-Israeli conflict, the South African Apartheid problem etc. Throughout the Free World and behind the Iron Curtain, new trouble-spots are continually appearing. How can a busy person like you get to know the real facts behind these events? And how can you be kept informed – swiftly and concisely – about tomorrow's trouble spots?

Up to now there has been no way. But now you can subscribe to an international news service which was designed to bring you, and thinking people like you, accurate and up-to-the-minute reports from all over the world.

INTELLIGENCE DIGEST SERVICE is a special private service based on top-level intelligence. You cannot buy it on the news-stands. It is circulated con-fidentially to subscribers only.

INTELLIGENCE DIGEST SERVICE gives you the facts about the international situation, and it concisely analyses their background. But, in addition, it guides you in advance about what is going to happen.

Our readers were forewarned about:

Devaluation of Sterling,
The fall of De Gaulle,
The Chinese-Russian Problem.

The Arab-Israeli War
Zambian Copper snatch

We have recently published important reports on:

1. South Africa and Britain – mutual interests (W/1/1)
2. South America: the gathering storm (D-Dec)
3. The Rhodesian Picture (D-Jan)
4. Brazil today (D-Jan)
5. Zambia's new brand of "democracy" (W/18/12)
6. June 1971: A month of protest (W/11/12)
   (See over for bonus offer.)

How has this been achieved?

For 32 years the publishers of INTELLIGENCE DIGEST SERVICE have specialised in this kind of top-level, behind-the-scenes-reporting. This information service was started and sponsored by an influential group of British Members of Parliament which, for the

Intelligence Digest

Cheltenham, England.

Dear Sir,

We believe that 1971 will be one of the most important years in history.

Each day brings news of some fresh crisis — economic difficulties in Britain and the U.S., new violence in the Arab-Israeli conflict, the South African Apartheid problem, etc. Throughout the Free World and behind the Iron Curtain, new trouble-spots are continually appearing. How can a busy person like you get to know the real facts behind these events? And how can you be kept informed — swiftly and concisely — about tomorrow's trouble spots?

Up to now there has been no way. But now you can subscribe to an international news service which was designed to bring you, and thinking people like you, accurate and up-to-the-minute reports from all over the world.

INTELLIGENCE DIGEST SERVICE is a special private service based on top-level intelligence. You cannot buy it on the news-stands. It is circulated confidentially to subscribers only.

INTELLIGENCE DIGEST SERVICE gives you the facts about the international situation, and it concisely analyses their background. But, in addition, it guides you in advance about what is going to happen.

Our readers were forewarned about:

Devaluation of Sterling,
The fall of De Gaulle,
The Chinese-Russian Problem.

We have recently published important reports on:

1. South Africa and Britain — mutual interests (W/1/1)
2. South America: the gathering storm (D-Dec)
3. The Rhodesian Picture (D-Jan)
4. Brazil today (D-Jan)
5. Zambia's new brand of "democracy" (W/18/12)
6. June 1971: A month of protest (W/11/12)

(See over for bonus offer.)

How has this been achieved?

For 32 years the publishers of INTELLIGENCE DIGEST SERVICE have specialised in this kind of top-level behind-the-scenes reporting. This information service was started and sponsored by an influential group of British Members of Parliament, which, for the

Now you can receive the best top-level inside information in the world.

You can now build up, week by week, a file of facts and figures — on international affairs — which are unobtainable elsewhere.

What does 1971 hold in store?

The Arab-Israeli War,
Zambian Copper snatch,

Now you can receive the best (top-level) inside information in the world.

Cheltenham, England.

Intelligence Digest

AND WEEKLY REVIEW

You can now build up, week by week, a file of facts and figures – on international affairs – which are unobtainable elsewhere.

Dear Sir,

What does 1971 hold in store?

We believe that 1971 will be one of the most (important) years in history.

Each day brings news of some fresh crisis – economic difficulties in Britain and the U.S., new violence in the Arab-Israeli conflict, the South African Apartheid problem, etc. Throughout the Free World and behind the Iron Curtain, new trouble-spots are continually appearing. How can a (busy person) like you get to know the real facts behind these events? And how can you be kept informed – swiftly and concisely – about tomorrow's trouble spots?

Up to now there has been no way. But now you can subscribe to an international news service which was designed to bring you, and (thinking people) like you, accurate and up-to-the-minute reports from all over the world.

INTELLIGENCE DIGEST SERVICE is a (special) private service based on (top-level) intelligence. You cannot buy it on the news-stands. It is circulated confidentially to subscribers only.

INTELLIGENCE DIGEST SERVICE gives you the facts about the international situation, and it concisely analyses their background. But, in addition, it guides you in advance about what is going to happen.

Our readers were forewarned about:

Devaluation of Sterling,
The fall of De Gaulle,
The Chinese-Russian Problem.

The Arab-Israeli War,
Zambian Copper snatch,

We have recently published important reports on:

1. South Africa and Britain – mutual interests (W/1/1)
2. South America: the gathering storm (D-Dec)
3. The Rhodesian Picture (D-Jan)
4. Brazil today (D-Jan)
5. Zambia's new brand of "democracy" (W/18/12)
6. June 1971: A month of protest (W/11/12)
   (See over for bonus offer)

How has this been achieved?

For 32 years the publishers of INTELLIGENCE DIGEST SERVICE have specialised in this kind of (top-level), behind-the-scenes-reporting. This information service was started and sponsored by an (influential group) of British (Members of Parliament) which, for the

(3) THINKING PEOPLE

Intelligence Digest

AND WEEKLY REVIEW

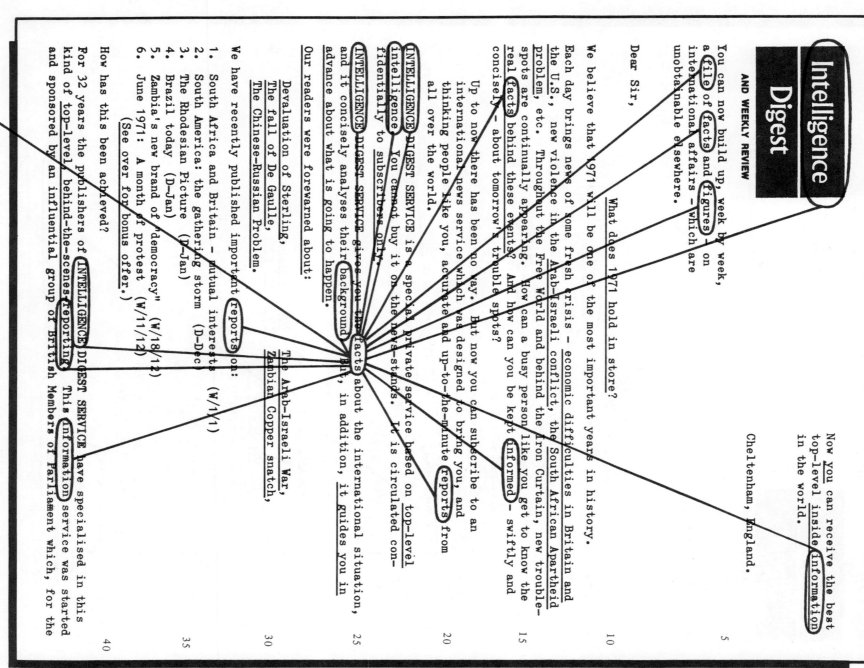

Now you can receive the best top-level inside (information) in the world.

Cheltenham, England.

Dear Sir,

You can now build up, week by week, a (file) of (facts) and (figures) — on international affairs — which are unobtainable elsewhere.

We believe that 1971 will be one of the most important years in history.

<u>What does 1971 hold in store?</u>

Each day brings news of some fresh crisis — economic difficulties in Britain and the U.S., new violence in the Arab-Israeli conflict, the <u>South African Apartheid problem</u>, etc. Throughout the Free World and behind the Iron Curtain, new trouble-spots are continually appearing. How can a busy person like you get to know the <u>real (facts)</u> behind these events? And how can you be kept (informed) — swiftly and concisely — about tomorrow's trouble spots?

Up to now there has been no way. But now you can subscribe to an international news service which was designed to bring you, and thinking people like you, accurate and up-to-the-minute (reports) from all over the world.

(INTELLIGENCE DIGEST SERVICE) is a special private service based on <u>top-level intelligence</u>. You cannot buy it on the news-stands. It is circulated confidentially to (subscribers only).

(INTELLIGENCE DIGEST SERVICE) gives you the (facts) about the international situation, and it concisely analyses their (background). But, in addition, <u>it guides you in advance</u> about what is going to happen.

Our readers were forewarned about:

Devaluation of Sterling,
The fall of De Gaulle,
The Chinese-Russian Problem.

We have recently published important (reports) on:

1. South Africa and Britain — mutual interests (w/1/1)
2. South America: the gathering storm (D-Jan)
3. The Rhodesian Picture (D-Jan)
4. Brazil today (D-Jan)
5. Zambia's new brand of "democracy" (w/18/12)
6. June 1971: A month of protest (w/11/12)
   (See over for bonus offer.)

The Arab-Israeli War,
Zambian Copper snatch,

How has this been achieved?

For 32 years the publishers of (INTELLIGENCE DIGEST SERVICE) have specialised in this kind of <u>top-level, behind-the-scenes (reporting)</u>. This (information) service was started and sponsored by an influential group of British Members of Parliament which, for the

(4) FACTS

5

10

15

20

25

30

35

40

Intelligence Digest

AND WEEKLY REVIEW

You can now build up, week by week,
a file of facts and figures – on
international affairs – which are
unobtainable elsewhere.

Cheltenham, England.

Dear Sir,

We believe that 1971 will be one of the most important years in history. What does 1971 hold in store?

Each day brings news of some fresh crisis – economic difficulties in Britain and the U.S., new violence in the Arab-Israeli conflict, the South African Apartheid problem, etc. Throughout the Free World and behind the Iron Curtain, new trouble-spots are continually appearing. How can a busy person like you get to know the real facts behind these events? And how can you be kept informed – swiftly and concisely – about tomorrow's trouble spots?

Up to now there has been no way. But now you can subscribe to an international news service which was designed to bring you, and thinking people like you, accurate and up-to-the-minute reports from all over the world.

INTELLIGENCE DIGEST SERVICE is a special private service based on top-level intelligence. You cannot buy it on the news-stands. It is circulated confidentially to subscribers only.

INTELLIGENCE DIGEST SERVICE gives you the facts about the international situation, and it concisely analyses their background. But, in addition, it guides you in advance about what is going to happen.

Our readers were forewarned about:

Devaluation of Sterling,
The fall of De Gaulle,
The Chinese-Russian Problem.

The Arab-Israeli War,
Zambian Copper snatch,

We have recently published important reports on:

1. South Africa and Britain – mutual interests (W/1/1)
2. South America: the gathering storm (D-Dec)
3. The Rhodesian Picture (D-Jan)
4. Brazil today (D-Jan)
5. Zambia's new brand of "democracy" (W/18/12)
6. June 1971: A month of protest (W/11/12)
   (See over for bonus offer.)

How has this been achieved?

For 32 years the publishers of INTELLIGENCE DIGEST SERVICE have specialised in this kind of top-level, behind-the-scenes-reporting. This information service was started and sponsored by an influential group of British Members of Parliament which, for the

Now you can receive the best
top-level inside information
in the world.

(5a) GIVES YOU

(5b) ANALYSES

68

The following passage from T. S. Eliot's poem, "The Love Song of
J. Alfred Prufrock", presents a number of highly probable collocations,
such as "rubs . . . back" and "licked . . . tongue". It also presents a
number of unusual collocations, such as "rubs . . . back . . . window-
panes" and "corners . . . evening".

The *yellow fog* that *rubs its back* upon the *window-panes*,
The *yellow smoke* that *rubs its muzzle* on the *window-panes*
Licked its *tongue* into the *corners* of the *evening*,
Lingered upon the *pools* that *stand* in *drains*,
Let *fall* upon its *back* the *soot* that *falls* from *chimneys*,
Slipped by the *terrace*, made a *sudden leap*,
And *seeing* that it was a *soft October night*,
Curled once about the *house*, and *fell asleep*.

EXERCISES:

1. List other unusual collocations. (To make this easier, the passage is
printed with all lexical items in italics.)

2. "Smog" constitutes an important lexical set. So does "house" and
"animal". List the items in these three lexical sets.

3. Write a short essay describing the smog. Take into account the inter-
action of the three major lexical sets.

Part Two

Diatypic Varieties

—Field of Discourse
—Mode of Discourse
—Personal Tenor of Discourse
—Functional Tenor of Discourse

FIELD OF DISCOURSE

Lexical patterning is concerned with an internal formal feature — the distribution of lexical items in a given text.

Field of discourse is concerned with another sort of patterning — the relationship between lexical items (language features) and the interest of the speaker (a non-language feature). What we are looking at, then, is a correlation.

A field of discourse can be technical or non-technical. The average guide employed at Upper Canada Village might be expected to spend much of the time speaking in the field of history, although the language he used would be less technically marked than that of a professional historian delivering a paper on Upper Canada Village to his learned colleagues.

In the concept "field of discourse", a scale of delicacy may be employed. For example, the professional historian discussing Upper Canada Village might be expected (at the lowest, or least delicate, level) to speak in the field *Canadian history*; at a more delicate level, in the subfield *Canadian history of the nineteenth century*; and, after proceeding through intermediary levels, might reach as high, or delicate, a level as the subfield *influences of British ore-refining techniques upon the hand crafting of horse-shoe nails during the years 1837 to 1838.*

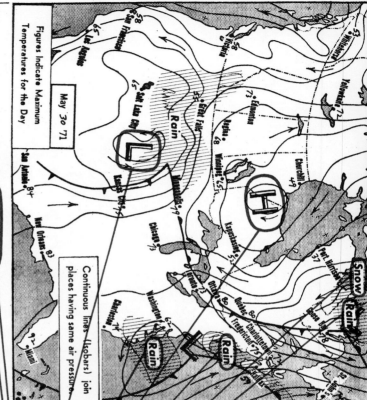

Figures Indicate Maximum Temperatures for the Day

May 30 71

Continuous lines (isobars) join places having same air pressure.

WEATHER

In "The Weather", the field of discourse is *weather*. It is marked most strongly by lexis, but the graphology is important, too. The letters "H" and "L" are *field restricted* — only in this field of discourse do they collocate with each other, but not with other letters of the alphabet. This collocation is so well established that they do not need to be glossed. The lines surrounding them are also field restricted. This particular use of graphic resources is less familiar, and therefore a double glossing is provided. First, they are defined in familiar terms ("Continuous lines ... join places having the same air pressure"); in addition, they are referred to as "isobars", a term by which they are known in the technical language of weather forecasting.

THE WEATHER

TORONTO: Mostly sunny. High 69 to 75. Tomorrow: Cloudy periods.

HAMILTON, LONDON, WINDSOR, LAKE ST. CLAIR, LAKE ERIE, LAKE HURON, NIAGARA, LAKE ONTARIO, HALIBURTON, SOUTHERN GEORGIAN BAY: Mostly sunny. High in the 60s to low 70s except around Lake St. Clair. Tomorrow: Cloudy periods.

NORTH BAY, SUDBURY, NORTHERN GEORGIAN BAY, ALGOMA, WHITE RIVER, COCHRANE: Sunny. High near 80. Tomorrow: Cloudy periods.

WESTERN JAMES BAY: Mainly cloudy except in areas bordering Hudson Bay. High near 60. Tomorrow: Sunny.

MONTREAL, OTTAWA, QUEBEC CITY, EASTERN TOWNSHIPS: Sunny with cloudy periods. High 70 to 75. Tomorrow: Cloudy periods.

At Toronto Airport
Yesterday's temperatures 8 a.m. 54; noon 71; 2 p.m. 72; 4 p.m. 72; 8 p.m. 72.
Maximum to 8 p.m. 74; minimum to 8 p.m. 49; mean 57; difference from average 3 below.
Wind: 8 a.m. WNW2 noon calm 8 p.m. N14.
Barometer: 8 a.m. 29.96; noon 29.92; 8 p.m. 29.82.
Rainfall to 8 p.m. nil; Saturday's maximum 71; Saturday's minimum 39; Saturday's rainfall nil.

TORONTO RECORDS

At Bloor Street Observatory
Yesterday's high 73; low 50; rainfall nil.
Saturday's high 71; low 50; rainfall to 8 p.m. nil.

At Toronto Island
Yesterday's high 68; low 44; rainfall to 8 p.m. nil.
Sun rises at 5:40; sets at 8:51.
Highest ever recorded in Toronto on May 31: 92 in 1895; lowest 33 in 1854.
Maximum and minimum for May 31 last year: 77 and 60.

TEMPERATURES

Temperatures at noon yesterday:

City	Low	High
Dawson	35	63
Prince George	48	56
Vancouver	50	60
Victoria	45	58
Jasper	45	69
Edmonton	48	73
Calgary	47	75
Yellowknife	50	72
Saskatoon	47	72
Regina	44	69
Winnipeg	31	65
Churchill	29	49
Thunder Bay	42	58
Sault Ste. Marie	42	61
Kapuskasing	40	52
Sudbury	44	76
Muskoka	37	75
Windsor	46	81
London	41	77
Peterborough	38	80
Kingston	43	71
Ottawa	50	80
Montreal	51	78
Quebec City	44	80
Fredericton	44	75
Halifax	45	59
Charlottetown	49	72
Sydney	50	74
St. John's	37	74
Minneapolis	59	79
Chicago	57	73
Buffalo	48	76
Boston	52	55
New York	54	61
Washington	54	62
Pittsburgh	48	78
Atlanta	49	75
Tampa	62	82
Miami	71	92
Orlando	66	86
New Orleans	57	83
St. Louis	49	78
Denver	39	70
Tucson	51	86
Los Angeles	59	65
San Francisco	48	58
Honolulu	70	80
Acapulco	79	86
Barbados	77	86
Bermuda	73	76
Kingston	57	77
Nassau	78	88
St. Kitts	76	85
San Juan	76	90

Temperatures at noon yesterday GMT: Aberdeen 52, Amsterdam 68, Ankara 77, Auckland 57, Berlin 63, Birmingham 63, Brussels 66, Casablanca 66, Copenhagen 57, Dublin 57, Geneva 63, Hong Kong 82, Lisbon 68, London 59, Madrid 70, Malta 70, Manila 86, Moscow 79, New Delhi 84, Nice 68, Oslo 55, Paris 61, Rome 66, Sofia 61, Stockholm 79, Tel Aviv 86, Tokyo 66, Tunis 77, Vienna 63, Warsaw 70.

EXERCISES:

1. Discuss the appropriateness of providing the term "isobars". Will it aid readers of the map?

2. High and low are lexical items used in discussing both air temperature and air pressure. What prevents their being confused?

3. Contrast the language of "The Weather" with that of "Toronto Records".

4. Use "The 60s" (the term for the previous decade), in a short paragraph of film criticism. Analyse what you have written to show how the field of discourse is established.

In "Sunny tomorrow" the field of discourse is also *weather*.

1. What is the collocation of "sunny" and "cloudy" in "Sunny tomorrow" and in "The Weather" (page 72)?

2. "Sunny tomorrow" has a greater range of subfields than "The Weather".

   (a) List the subfields of this text.

   (b) Discuss the ways in which the overall effects of the two texts differ.

Sunny tomorrow
high of 70 expected
low tonight near 45

Weather

TORONTO FORECAST

Wednesday mostly sunny. Low tonight near 45, high tomorrow near 70.

POLLUTION INDEX

The air pollution index at 11 a.m. was 10 in Toronto, 21 in Hamilton, 13 in Sudbury, and 7 in Windsor. The index measures two of many pollutants in the air. Readings below 32 are regarded as satisfactory; above 58, harmful to the health of some persons.

TORONTO CALENDAR

Sunrise 5.39 a.m.
Sunset 8.52 p.m.
High yesterday at 3.20 p.m. 65.
Low yesterday at 5.00 a.m. 55.
Low today up to 7 a.m.; was at 4.00 a.m. 48.
High since 1841 was in 1895, 92.
Low since 1841 was in 1854, 35.
A year ago: High 81, low 65.
Mean yesterday 60.1 below normal.
Humidity at 7 a.m. 68%.
Barometer 30.13 and rising.
Phase of the Moon:
Moon First Quarter: Rises 1.26 p.m.
Visible planets, evening Venus, Mars, Jupiter, Saturn.

ONTARIO OUTLOOK

The fine summer weather Ontario has enjoyed for the past three days will continue for two more days at least with sunny skies and temperatures in the sixties today and slightly higher tomorrow. The only dark spot is extreme Southwestern Ontario where cloudy skies and some showers are expected.

OTHER PROVINCES

B.C. cloudy; Alberta cloudy, intermittent rain; Saskatchewan and Manitoba sunny; Quebec sunny; Maritimes sunny; Newfoundland, c l o u d y, rain and drizzle.

U.S. WEATHER

Showers and thunderstorms are predicted for a large part of the north and central western regions. Variable cloudiness and warm weather will occur from southern California to the southern plains. Pleasant weather will extend from New England to the lower Mississippi valley.

OVERSEAS

Latest available observations:
Aberdeen, 46, cloudy; Athens, 66, cloudy; Berlin, 57, clear; Cairo, 66, clear; Dublin, 55 cloudy; Hong Kong, 82, rain; London, 54, cloudy; Madrid, 57, clear; Manila, 82, cloudy; Moscow 54, clear; New Delhi, 82, cloudy; Paris, 57, cloudy; Rome 59, clear; Saigon, 79, cloudy; Stockholm 55, clear; Sydney, 55, clear; Tel Aviv 59, cloudy; Tokyo, 70 cloudy; Warsaw, 64, cloudy; Buenos Aires, 59, clear; Rio de Janeiro 70, clear.

TEMPERATURES

	Low night	High yesterday
Dawson	55	68
Prince George	37	59
Prince Rupert	43	54
Vancouver	52	62
Victoria	49	62
Jasper	41	66
Edmonton	37	65
Calgary	40	49
Lethbridge	43	48
Yellowknife	44	69
Prince Albert	44	74
Saskatoon	45	71
Regina	39	70
Winnipeg	35	70
Churchill	29	48
Thunder Bay	29	55
White River	32	69
Kapuskasing	34	62
Earlton	32	62
North Bay	37	59
Sudbury	38	61
Sault Ste. Marie	32	58
Muskoka	35	65
Windsor	50	69
London	47	67
Kingston	38	67
Peterborough	34	65
Killaloe	27	63
Ottawa	43	64
Montreal	38	65
Quebec city	36	65
Fredericton	42	72
Saint John	45	67
Moncton	45	65
Halifax	52	61
Charlottetown	43	62
Sydney	42	62
Yarmouth	47	58
St. John's	52	63

U.S. POINTS

	Low night	High yesterday
Minneapolis	52	70
Bismarck	44	50
Chicago	56	58
Detroit	50	75
Buffalo	46	65
Albany	39	72
Boston	51	68
New York	55	71
Washington	59	83
Pittsburgh	53	81
Cincinnati	56	84
Raleigh	54	82
Atlanta	57	84
Jacksonville	62	88
Tampa	70	87
Miami	66	91
New Orleans	61	88
Orlando	66	87
Oklahoma City	62	90
St. Louis	64	84
Kansas City	45	89
Denver	61	74
Tucson	59	87
Los Angeles	54	65
San Francisco	50	59
Boise	48	67
Honolulu	73	83

There is considerable overlap in the lexis of "Winds" and that of the two weather reports. Consider the following lexical sets:

Good — bad weather: (fine, sunny, cloudy, pleasant, sluggish, torpid, oppressive).

Air as measurable: (air, pressure, wind, velocity, WNW2, calm, barometer, inches of mercury, high pressure, low, H, L).

Nevertheless, the language of "Winds" is clearly different from that of "Sunny tomorrow" (page 73) and of "The Weather" (page 72).

CHAPTER XXI

WINDS

Wind is air in approximately horizontal motion. Observations of the wind should include its true direction, and its force or velocity. The direction of the wind is designated by the point of the compass from which it proceeds. The force of the wind is at sea ordinarily expressed in terms of the Beaufort scale, each degree of this scale corresponding to a certain velocity in nautical or statute miles per hour, as explained in chapter II, or it may also be expressed directly in nautical or statute miles per hour.

The cause of wind.—Winds are produced by differences of atmospheric pressure, which are for the most part primarily attributable to differences of temperature.

To understand how the air can be set in motion by these differences of pressure, it is necessary to have a clear conception of the nature of air itself.

The atmosphere which completely envelops the earth may be considered a sea of air at the bottom of which we live. It extends upward to a considerable height, the density constantly diminishing as the altitude increases, but being still appreciable at 150 to 200 miles or more.

The air is a mixture of transparent gases which, like all gases, is elastic and highly compressible. Although extremely light, it has a definite weight which can be measured. A cubic foot of air at ordinary pressure and temperature weighs 1.22 ounces, or about one seven hundred and seventieth part of the weight of an equal volume of water. In consequence of this weight the air exerts a certain pressure upon the surface of the earth, amounting on the average to 15 pounds per square inch. To accurately measure this pressure, which is constantly undergoing slight changes, a mercurial barometer is used (ch. II). This is an instrument in which the weight of a column of mercury is balanced against the weight of the outside air pressing against the column at one end. The height of the column of mercury which the weight of the air will support at any particular time and place is called the atmospheric or barometric pressure at that time and place. Instead of saying that the pressure of the atmosphere is a certain number of pounds per square inch, it is customary to say that it is a certain number of inches of mercury, meaning that a column of air of given cross section extending from the barometer to the upper limit of the atmosphere supports a column of mercury of the same cross section and the stated number of inches in height.

When air that is not confined is heated, it increases in volume. When cooled, its volume is diminished. Suppose now that the atmosphere over any considerable

5

10

15

20

25

30

EXERCISES:

1. In paragraph 5, to what lexical set do "transparent gases", "elastic", "volume", and "pressure" belong?

2. Find other items in this lexical set.

3. What field of discourse does this set establish?

SOCIOLOGY

SCIENCE

5 SOCIOLOGY: ITS PRESENT INTERESTS

Harry Alpert

Harry Alpert, Dean of the Graduate School at the University of Oregon, was born in New York City in 1912. A specialist in research methodology, social psychology, and inter-relations of the natural and social sciences, Dr. Alpert took his academic training at the College of the City of New York, the University of Bordeaux, France, and Columbia University. He has taught on the faculties of the College of the City of New York, Yale University, Queens College, the American University, and the University of Washington. He is a former President of the American Association for Public Opinion Research (1955) and is the author of many articles and books, including Emile Durkheim and His Sociology.

To George Bernard Shaw is attributed the remark that America's youth is its oldest tradition. The observation is applicable with equal cogency to sociology, the science of society. Many of the limitations of sociology are frequently excused on the ground that it is a very young discipline. And, indeed, as scientific studies go, sociology is quite youthful: just 120 years old, if we may date its origin, somewhat arbitrarily, from the first appearance of the newly-coined word "sociology" in the forty-seventh chapter of Auguste Comte's *The Positive Philosophy*. Comte invented this barbaric cognomen in order to designate by a specialized name the scientific study of the fundamental laws of social phenomena.

Although sociology had its birth in the nineteenth century, chiefly in response to the immediate practical requirements of social reconstruction and societal amelioration, its major contemporary features—rigorous methodology, empirical emphasis, behavioral orientation, and conceptual consciousness—are largely a product of the past half-century.

In terms of its present interests, sociology may be defined as the scientific study of society, its structure, functions, and processes. In this over-all view of the discipline, I shall attempt to identify the general areas of sociological concern and comment briefly on selected specialized fields of sociological inquiry. Some of these special fields will be described in greater detail in later papers in this series.

In the broadest sense, sociology studies society in terms of its structure, organization, change, and relation to environment. Professor Robert M. MacIver's definition of the field is a useful formulation of the major interests of this discipline. "Sociology seeks to discover the principles of cohesion and of order within the social structure, the ways in which it roots and grows within an environment, the moving equilibrium of changing structure and changing environment, the main trends of this incessant change and the forces which determine its direction at any time, the harmonies and conflicts, the adjustments and maladjustments within the structure as they are revealed in the light of human desires, and thus the practical application of means to ends in the creative activities of social man."

As a scientific discipline, sociology may be divided into three broad, analytical fields: the study of groups; institutional analysis; and the study of social structure in general.

Group analysis is currently one of the fields of research in which sociologists are most active. Social groups are viewed as individuals regularly in contact or communication who, for certain purposes, identify themselves with each other. Small intimate groups may range from a family to a play group or a neighborhood. To distinguish such groups from larger and less closely associated aggregates, such as an urban community, some sociologists use the terms primary and secondary. Other sociologists have developed the concept of quasi-group to cover social classes, publics, and other aggregates or portions of the community which have no recognizable structure, but whose members have certain interests or

35

40

45

50

55

60

65

modes of behavior in common which may at any time lead 70
them to form themselves into definite groups. The nature
and types of social groupings, the bases of group formation,
the processes of group cohesion, the conditions of group action, and the structure and patterns of intergroup relations
are among the major problems with which this area of soci- 75
ology is concerned.

Suggestive ideas have been developed in analysis of group
behavior from a consideration of the way in which members
of the same group regard each other as against all outsiders.
This in-group versus out-group distinction has supplied clues 80
to the understanding of intergroup relations. The concepts,
first formulated by William Graham Sumner in his famous
Folkways, refer to the fact that group relations affect ethical
judgments and ways of thinking. Thus, a particular action by
a member of one's own political party will be viewed as an 85
excusable error, while the same act by a member of the op-
position is deemed to be a gross betrayal of trust. An extreme
form of group attitude is represented by ethnocentrism,
which is the view of things in which one's own group is the
center of everything and all others are scaled with reference 90
to it.

But ethnocentrism is only one aspect of the process by
which groups develop conceptions of themselves and of
others. Group images, that is, the typical mental pictures that
members have of themselves and others, serve to define their 95
relations to one another and play an important part in determining the nature of intergroup contacts. In this connection,
the study of stereotypes or fixed mental images is especially
important.

Social groups have also been analyzed as "sifting devices" 100
whereby people in a large urban population are organized in
associations having recognized positions of prestige or power,
such as churches, exclusive clubs, or boards of directors. The
role of groups in determining the status and power structure
of modern American communities is effectively presented in 105

the *Yankee City* series directed by Professor W. Lloyd War- 110
ner. Professor Robert S. Lynd, among others, has analyzed
power relations in American society, but in general the study
of who belongs to what, for what reason, and with what effect
is still in its early stages.

Recent research on industrial morale, clique behavior,
voting behavior, consumer buying, sociometric patterns, and 115
group dynamics has tended to reaffirm the sociological conception of the influential character of the small, direct, face-
to-face group and has increased understanding of the nature
of interpersonal relations in the small group. Professor Paul
F. Lazarsfeld and his associates at Columbia University have
made significant contributions in this area.

Institutions are a second major field of sociological inter- 120
est. Institutions are variously defined by the different social
sciences, but the accent among sociologists is on an organized
system of practices and actions and the machinery evolved to
maintain the system of rules or norms of expected behavior.
Institutions are seen as established, determinate forms in ac- 125
cordance with which men enter into relations with one another. The major social institutions such as marriage, kin-
ship, law, property, education, religion, recreation, welfare,
art, science, health, government, warfare, and political and
economic institutions are the subject of specialized sociologi- 130
cal disciplines (sociology of law, sociology of religion, sociology of art, sociology of the family, and so forth).

Among the numerous ideas that have developed from institutional analysis, the following five may be singled out for
special mention: the persistence of certain basic institutions 135
like the family as universal features of social organization;
the transference and shifting of functions over time from one
institution to another, such as the transfer of welfare functions from the family to the state; the interdependence of
institutions so that changes in one create changes in others; 140
the operation of a principle of congeniality or a "strain
towards consistency" among institutions in a given society;

At the lowest level of delicacy, the field of discourse of "Sociology: Its Present Interests": is *science*. The word "science" itself is one marker: others are lexical items like "research" which are commonly found in this field. In this text, the lowest level of delicacy is not very important. It is not heavily marked, and terms at this level of delicacy are not glossed.

At higher delicacy, the subfield *behavioral science* is hardly marked at all, but it is suggested by the lexical item "psychology" and the phrase "inter-relations of the natural and social sciences". (See paragraph in italic type.)

At a yet higher level of delicacy, the subfield of the *science of sociology*, the text is definitely marked by the consistent use of field restricted lexis. This field restriction is achieved by collocation and glossing.

The lexical item "social", for example, can occur in a variety of collocations: "social page", "social graces", "church social", "socialized medicine", "social conscience", and "social climber".

At the beginning of the text, many of these possibilities are eliminated. "Social", the root word of sociology, is shown through its collocation with other scientific terms to have a special "field restricted" meaning. (Note its occurrence in the second sentence of the passage in italics: "A specialist in research methodology, *social* psychology, and inter-relations of the natural and *social* sciences, Dr. Alpert took his academic training at the College of . . .") In each case, "social" collocates with a lexical item which is clearly scientific: "social *psychology*" and "social *sciences*".

The second of these ("sciences") relates the subfield to the overall field, while the first ("psychology") establishes "social" in the subfield by relating it to another behavioural science. Other items in the sentence establishing the overall field (science) are "specialist", "research", and "methodology".

Field restriction is also achieved by the overt glossings "the science of society" (line 17), "the study of the fundamental laws of social phenomena" (line 26), and "the scientific study of society, its structure, functions, and processes" (line 34). The paragraph beginning at line 40 provides an extended overt gloss.

While the field "science" and the subfield "sociology" continue to be marked throughout the text, at line 57 the text becomes marked at a higher level of delicacy for another subfield within sociology, the *group*.

80

"Group" is defined by specific modification. It is introduced as part of a qualifier ("the study of *groups*"), and then occurs as a nominal modifier ("*group* analysis"), but the real work of definition is done as the word "group" appears at the head position ("social *groups*", "small intimate *groups*", "a family to a play *group*", and, finally, the phrase "such *groups*"). At this point the lexical item "group" is carefully and formally distinguished from "aggregates".

Once "group" has been established as a term, it begins to float about in phrase structure, occurring now as modifier ("*group* relations") and now as part of a qualifier ("interpersonal relations *in the small group*").

EXERCISES:

1. The text, *Sociology: Its Present Interests* has "science" and "the science of sociology" as field and subfield of discourse throughout. On *each* of the four pages of text, find markers indicating this field and subfield.

2. The text is very clearly structured. Show how the author explicitly introduces the subfield "group", and as explicitly indicates that he has finished with it.

3. Indicate what subfields can be established by analysis at yet higher delicacy within "group". (Note that these often coincide with the graphological unit "paragraph".)

For many people, the "Vectors" text will be difficult to read. Precisely because it is unintelligible (to the general reader), it allows us to take an objective look at its language. Even if we don't know exactly what it means, we can say a great deal about how its language works. A glance reveals that the text is unmistakably marked at the graphological level for the field of mathematics.

EXERCISES:

1. Analyse the "Vectors" text into field at as many levels of delicacy as you can. (At low delicacy the field remains constant, while at higher delicacy, field shifts occur.)

2. "Vectors" is a teaching text which is carefully introducing new field restricted terms.

(a) Find and list the terms which are being introduced as new terms.

(b) Discuss the type of definition which is used to explain them.

(c) Why are the explanation unsatisfactory for the general reader?

46 VECTORS [CHAP. 1

ANSWERS

2. (a) $5\mathbf{i} + 2\mathbf{k}$, (b) $\mathbf{i} - 3\mathbf{j}$, (c) 2, (d) 2, (e) $\frac{\sqrt{15}}{30}$, (f) 3,
(g) $\sqrt{3}$, (h) 1, −1, 1, (i) $\frac{\sqrt{6}}{3}$, (j) $\frac{\sqrt{10}}{10}$, (k) $\frac{4\sqrt{3}}{3}$, (l) $-4\mathbf{i} + 2\mathbf{j} + 6\mathbf{k}$.

3. (a) −1, −1, −2, (b) $\sqrt{6}$, (c) 4, (d) arc cos $(4/\sqrt{66})$, (e) $\frac{1}{2}\sqrt{50}$.

4. $\frac{3\sqrt{14}}{7}$

5. (a) 3, −1, 1, (b) $\frac{3}{\sqrt{11}}, -\frac{1}{\sqrt{11}}, \frac{1}{\sqrt{11}}$.

6. (a) $\overrightarrow{P_1P} \cdot \mathbf{b} = 0$ (b) $b_z(x - x_1) + b_y(y - y_1) + b_z(z - z_1) = 0$.

7. $x + y - 4z = 5$. 8. (a) $\overrightarrow{OP} \cdot \mathbf{b} = p$, (b) $lx + my + nz = p$.

9. $\frac{2x+y+2z}{3} = 3$. 10. $d^2 = a^2 - \frac{(\mathbf{a} \cdot \mathbf{b})^2}{b^2}$, $\mathbf{a} = \overrightarrow{P_1P_2}$, $\mathbf{b} = \overrightarrow{P_2P_3}$.

11. $\frac{1}{2}\sqrt{6}$. 12. 6 ft-lb.

1-10 Orientation in space. The notions of right-handed and left-handed systems of axes are familiar in analytic geometry. It is assumed in this book that right-handed systems are used.

Let $\mathbf{i}, \mathbf{j}, \mathbf{k}$ denote a fixed triple of unit vectors, corresponding to a fixed choice of a (right-handed) xyz coordinate system. This triple of unit vectors, in the given order, will be called a *positive triple*.

If $\mathbf{i}_1, \mathbf{j}_1, \mathbf{k}_1$ is any other triple of mutually perpendicular vectors in space, then the triple $\mathbf{i}_1, \mathbf{j}_1, \mathbf{k}_1$ in that order is called a positive triple if it is possible to move the triple $\mathbf{i}, \mathbf{j}, \mathbf{k}$ rigidly through space into coincidence with the triple $\mathbf{i}_1, \mathbf{j}_1, \mathbf{k}_1$, $\mathbf{i}$ going to $\mathbf{i}_1$, $\mathbf{j}$ to $\mathbf{j}_1$, $\mathbf{k}$ to $\mathbf{k}_1$, as in Fig. 1–18. Thus $\mathbf{i}_1, \mathbf{j}_1, \mathbf{k}_1$ could also serve as the basis of a right-handed coordinate system. If $\mathbf{i}_1, \mathbf{j}_1, \mathbf{k}_1$ is not a positive triple, then it will be called a *negative triple*.

It follows from this that the triples $(\mathbf{i}, \mathbf{j}, \mathbf{k})$, $(\mathbf{k}, \mathbf{i}, \mathbf{j})$, $(\mathbf{j}, \mathbf{k}, \mathbf{i})$ are all positive, while the triples $(\mathbf{j}, \mathbf{i}, \mathbf{k})$, $(\mathbf{k}, \mathbf{j}, \mathbf{i})$, $(\mathbf{i}, \mathbf{k}, \mathbf{j})$ are all negative. Thus it is only the cyclic order which counts.

This notion can be extended to an arbitrary triple $(\mathbf{a}, \mathbf{b}, \mathbf{c})$ of non-coplanar vectors. For it is possible to distort such a triple into a triple $(\mathbf{a}', \mathbf{b}', \mathbf{c}')$ of mutually perpendicular vectors by rotating the vectors through acute angles, without having one of the vectors cross the plane of the other two. The triple $(\mathbf{a}', \mathbf{b}', \mathbf{c}')$ can now be replaced by a system of unit vectors $(\mathbf{i}_1, \mathbf{j}_1, \mathbf{k}_1)$ having the same respective directions. The triple $(\mathbf{a}, \mathbf{b}, \mathbf{c})$ is called positive if $(\mathbf{i}_1, \mathbf{j}_1, \mathbf{k}_1)$ is positive, and is negative otherwise; it can be shown that the result here is independent of the particular manner in which $(\mathbf{a}, \mathbf{b}, \mathbf{c})$ is distorted into the triple $(\mathbf{a}', \mathbf{b}', \mathbf{c}')$. As before, it is only the cyclic order which counts, so that if $(\mathbf{a}, \mathbf{b}, \mathbf{c})$ is positive, then so are $(\mathbf{b}, \mathbf{c}, \mathbf{a})$ and $(\mathbf{c}, \mathbf{a}, \mathbf{b})$, while $(\mathbf{b}, \mathbf{a}, \mathbf{c})$, etc., are negative. Furthermore, it is easily seen that if $(\mathbf{a}, \mathbf{b}, \mathbf{c})$ is positive, then $(\mathbf{a}, \mathbf{b}, -\mathbf{c})$ is negative.

The choice of a preferred type of coordinate system (the right-handed system), with a corresponding grouping of triples of vectors into the two

81

MODE OF DISCOURSE

Language is manifested either as patterned marks on paper or as patterned vibrations in air. The language user's choice of medium makes a considerable difference to the language produced: a speaker has resources (intonation patterns, tempo, length of pause, stress, et cetera) different from those utilized by the writer (formal or casual handwriting, underlinings, punctuation marks, italic type, upper and lower case letters, et cetera). Language exists, then, in either the *spoken mode* or the *written mode*. (When a person uses both sounds and marks simultaneously, for instance by writing a sentence on a blackboard while speaking it, he is creating two texts, one in the *spoken mode* and one in the *written mode*.) There are, however, distinctions which can be shown *within* each mode, and there are relationships *between* the two modes.

I SPOKEN MODE

The spoken mode may be *spontaneous* or *nonspontaneous*.

Spontaneous speech, that is speech in which the actual lexical and grammatical choices are made on the spot, is again divided into *conversing* and *monologuing*.

Monologuing is the speaking by one individual in such a way as to exclude the possibility of interruption by others. *Conversing* is speaking in such a way as to invite the participation of others. It is quite possible for one person to converse at another and be the only speaker; he need only ask a series of genuine questions, for example, without receiving an answer. Similarly two people can monologue at each other. Try listening to a conversation between crushing bores at a social gathering, for an example of this phenomenon.

Nonspontaneous spoken speech may consist of *reciting*, or the speaking exactly of material which has never been written. This is not a major mode in our society, being manifested mainly in certain varieties of children's language. In our culture, most nonspontaneous speech is the *speaking of what is written*. This is not limited to plays; anything which has been written, even a telephone book, may be spoken.

II WRITTEN MODE

The script from which an actor learns his lines is language in the written mode, but the author of this script attempts to represent spontaneous speech. The modality of such language is more delicately described as *written to be spoken as if not written*.

The script for a speech will also be written with its delivery in mind. Although the writer will take into account the way in which it will be delivered, he will not usually attempt to conceal its written origin. Such language may be described as *written to be spoken*.

There remains language *written not necessarily to be spoken*. Such language may bear no appreciable relation to the spoken mode; for example, the telephone book mentioned above, or a dictionary. Such language is more delicately described as *written to be read*.

Language may be written not necessarily to be spoken, but with a relationship to the spoken mode; for example, the dialogue in a novel, *to be read as speech*.

Related to this, because it implies a person "making" the language, is the interior monologue, *to be read as if thought*. This mode is widely used in modern fiction.

It is not usually the practice to categorize elaborately the dialogue in a novel as in the mode *written, not necessarily to be spoken, to be read as speech*. The final distinction, *to be read as speech*, is enough.

Table 1:   The Spoken Mode

Spoken language may be:

(1)   Spontaneous, which may be
     — Conversing
     — Monologuing

(2)   Nonspontaneous, which may be
     — Reciting
     — Speaking what is written. (The written text may be *any* of the types in table 2.)

Table 2:   The Written Mode

Written language may be:

(1)   Written to be spoken as if not written

(2)   Written to be spoken

(3)   Written not necessarily to be spoken
     — written to be read
     — written to be read as speech
     — written to be read as thought

SPOKEN MODE: SPONTANEOUS SPEECH — CONVERSING AND MONOLOGUING

Below is a transcript of spontaneous speech. In its transition to the written mode, it has lost many markers, but it is still easily identifiable.

The text is spontaneous speech containing passages in each of the two submodes "conversing" and "monologuing". The conversing passages can be distinguished by the larger number of minor clauses and by the presence of response-seeking words and constructions. The monologuing passages are characterized by devices to exclude interruption.

B Well speed reading um . . . you . . . to be perfect you have to read sixteen
    pages . . . in one minute . . .   5
G Oooh boy . . .
G That's hard . . .
B (overlapping) about um thousands of words I don't know. They're real
    thin . . . letters . . . an . . you're they're I don't know . . . how many
    thousands of words . . . you read . . .
G I
B Well I was watching this show and um there was this lady and he kept on . . .   10
    flipping the pages like this . . .
G Um . . . most people lic lick their fingers to . . .
B Ya
G to wet the page
G I don't lick the pages I sit there an I struggle an sometimes I (laughter)
    I rip the page in the book . . . uh . . . Have any o Heather did you watch   15
    any TV last night?
G Ya
G What
G Well it was a um . . . what's it called uh
G That Girl?
G No . . . it's some program that's on channel six That's a Girl is . . .   20
    (unintelligible) . . .
G He and She?
G Ya (overlapping)
G Oh . . . oh I watch that sometimes . . . and there's Andrew that that
    plumbing man an then there's . . . (?) Henry he's the fire man an he comes   25
    out the fire on the fire ladder all the time and every time . . . I saw um
    when he they when um . . . um Paula and um what's his . . . Dick Paula an
    Dick were . . getting . . . their second married because the first time
    they got married it wasn't very nice . . . and like Henry was the best
    man and he was han he was just about to hand the ring ta . . . to um . . .   30
    Dick . . . when um th the fire alarm sounded and he ran down the ladder an
    they had no time to us and then you see there was this um the man

EXERCISES:

1. Find markers of spontaneity in addition to the circled ones.

2. Describe any feature of this text which would make it difficult to
    interrupt the speaker.

SPOKEN MODE: SPONTANEOUS SPEECH — MONOLOGUING

The "Flamingo" text is highly marked in several ways. A phrase such as "Thus far you haven't seen" is unfamiliar, although it is difficult to say whether this is the result of the speaker's social or geographical dialect or a personal idiosyncrasy.

The markers of spontaneous monologuing stand out despite the text's strangeness in personal, social and geographical respects. Every sentence consists of a major clause. In its spoken form the text reveals what the transcript does not: a singsong pattern suggesting that it is a "patter" highly familiar to the speaker.

EXERCISE:

What markers of spontaneous monologuing are present in the transcript?

they were brought here .. when they were about three months old .. and as part of the experiments .. the flamingos and I .. when they were about four months . . . . we didn't know whether or not we would succeed .. and uh so it was done secretly . . . they were presented to the public only eleven years ago .. last March .. when his excellency the governor here . . . and a number of local and foreign dignitaries . . . came to see the first parade .. after fourteen months of experimenting . . . . the birds are in now over eleven years in training .. and I think they are doing very well indeed . . . . and very shortly now .. very shortly .. you will witness the most unique show .. thus far you haven't seen .. and may never never see anyplace else in the world . . . . and now t'give y'apreview .. of what's going to happen and uh so ya may be ready for it . . . the birds will come out of de water at command .. and then muster over there for a second . . obeying the command forward march by the right .. and as it were .. goose-step around the parade ground . . . in the buff for your close up view of dem . . . obeying command as they go by .. about turn .. equivalent to about face in the American army .. about turn over there or wherever you want them for that matter .. until they are in position . . they will mark time and stand easy for you .. while you take your pictures . . . . .

5

10

15

SPOKEN MODE: NONSPONTANEOUS — RECITING

These verses have been passed from one child to another on the playground. Their humour depends on interplay between the phonological and lexical levels. For example, the first line of the verse "I had an Auntie Nellie" sets up strong phonological expectations for a similar-sounding word at the end of the second line. The word "belly" is, therefore, entirely suitable in this respect. At the lexical level, however, the word "belly" violates the probabilities of collocational expectation: it is not a lexical item one expects to find immediately following "wooden". The simultaneous satisfaction and violation of expectations produce the humorous effect of the verse.

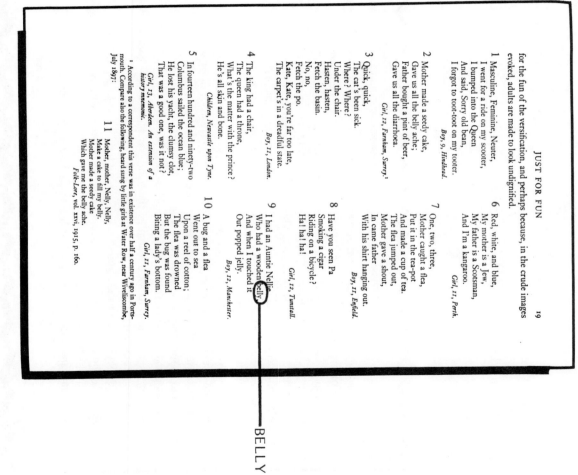

JUST FOR FUN

19

for the fun of the versification, and perhaps because, in the crude images evoked, adults are made to look undignified.

1 Masculine, Feminine, Neuter,
I went for a ride on my scooter,
I bumped into the Queen
And said, Sorry old bean,
I forgot to toot-toot on my tooter.

Boy, 9, Hindhead.

2 Mother made a seedy cake,
Gave us all the belly ache;
Father bought a pint of beer,
Gave us all the diarrhoea.

Girl, 12, Farnham, Surrey.

3 Quick, quick,
The cat's been sick.
Where? Where?
Under the chair.
Hasten, hasten,
Fetch the basin.
No, no,
Fetch the po.
Kate, Kate, you're far too late,
The carpet's in a dreadful state.

Boy, 11, London.

4 The king had a chair,
The queen had a throne,
What's the matter with the prince?
He's all skin and bone.

Children, Newcastle upon Tyne.

5 In fourteen hundred and ninety-two
Columbus sailed the ocean blue;
He lost his yacht, the clumsy clot,
That was a good one, was it not?

Girl, 13, Aberdeen. An extension of a history mnemonic.

6 Red, white, and blue,
My mother is a Jew,
My father is a Scotsman,
And I'm a kangaroo.

Girl, 11, Perth.

7 One, two, three,
Mother caught a flea,
Put it in the tea-pot
And made a cup of tea.
The flea jumped out,
Mother gave a shout,
In came father
With his shirt hanging out.

Boy, 11, Enfield.

8 Have you seen Pa
Smoking a cigar
Riding on a bicycle?
Ha! ha! ha!

Girl, 12, Tunstall.

9 I had an Auntie Nellie
Who had a wooden belly,
And when I touched it
Out popped jelly.

Boy, 12, Manchester.

10 A bug and a flea
Went out to sea
Upon a reel of cotton;
The flea was drowned
But the bug was found
Biting a lady's bottom.

Girl, 11, Farnham, Surrey.

11 Mother, mother, Nelly, Nelly,
Make a cake to fill my belly,
Mother made a seedy cake,
Which gave me the belly ache.

Folk-Lore, vol. xxvi, 1915, p. 160.

¹ According to a correspondent this verse was in existence over half a century ago in Portsmouth. Compare also the following, heard sung by little girls at Water Row, near Wiveliscombe, July 1897:

BELLY

EXERCISE:

Discuss the interplay between phonology and lexis in another of these verses.

WRITTEN MODE: WRITTEN TO BE SPOKEN

Below are excerpts from two speeches. Both were written to be spoken though they differ somewhat within this mode. Speech 1, by William Davis, makes no effort to conceal its written origin. Speech 2, by Douglas Wright, with its greater informality, is closer to ordinary spoken language. This effect is accomplished mainly at the lexical, but also at the grammatical, level.

est, however, as a reminder of what has happened during this last ten-year period and these have been set out as Appendix 'A' to this statement so that they may be reflected upon in a suitable fashion.

I might note, simply to give the dimensions of growth during the period, that from 1960 to 1970 enrolment has risen from 28,800 to 114,000, the number of universities have increased from 12 to 16, and the number of campuses to 21, the number of faculty have grown from 1830 to almost 8,000, and the support levels have risen from $15 million to $311 million annually on the operating side and from $12.7 million to $145 million in the capital area.

It seems fair to say that few, if any, would have predicted that type of development in 1960, and even fewer, had they heard such figures suggested, would have had confidence we could meet such targets. We did, and it should give us reassurance for the future.

Obviously we cannot measure, nor should we attempt to measure, the accomplishments in higher education in Ontario strictly in terms of numbers of students or in dollars expended. There are

Before leaving these notions, let me note the irony of the 19th century notion of liberal education in the 20th century when there is relatively so little wealth left to inherit. Somehow we must restructure university studies so that they may be both pro- fessional, in the sense of preparing people to contribute effectively,   5 and humane.

The great hangup of the American university is, of course, that no one has yet really properly sorted out the nature and proper uses of the power of the university which derives from knowledge and the ability to create new knowledge. As James Ridgeway in his re-   10 cent book, "The Closed Corporation", makes so clear, American uni- versities have been full of ineptitude, conflicts of interest and other improprieties, with no small slice of avarice, when they came to deal with the fruits of their creation. I wouldn't for a minute defend or rationalize the relationship of American universities to the military   15

- 8 -

with their Institutes of Defense Analysis and the like. But there is

a chicken and egg problem here because universities in the United

States as elsewhere consume wealth as well as creating it. In re-

sponse to the great pressure of young people who see university as

a route to the good life, universities have expanded immensely in 20

recent years. And at enormous cost.

The fact that knowledge is now the greatest source of wealth

and power and that universities in turn are the great sources of knowl-

edge is immutable. Those who rant and rave about universities in 25

the United States and Canada being too much involved in power are

naive: it cannot go away. But, if the efforts of the SDS and others

cause the universities and society to think out more clearly the uses

of the universities' power, then only good can come. For this power

must surely be used to benefit society at large. And moreover, there

is a clear need for more rather than less university involvement in 30

- 9 -

problem solving - but of the sort that improves the quality of life.

And let's not forget that a cheaper 'fridge to keep your beer cold

also improves the quality of your life.

This debate about the use of knowledge arises concurrently

with the challenge of authority which is affecting churches and gov-   35

ernments as well as universities. The basis of the challenge to

established authority is, of course, that right makes might. Real

power is vested in knowledge, now, rather than in any established

order. There is no little irony in the universities getting caught on

this one.

I see a related irony in the recent troubles in Mexico. It   40

has been my privilege to work some in Mexico. I have great respect

for the successes of the Mexican Revolution - their real revolution,

that is, that occurred in the decade following 1910, after almost a

century of what amounted to palace revolutions. There seem only   45

EXERCISES:

1. Find markers in Speech 1 establishing the text's written origin.

2. Find markers in Speech 2 giving a flavour of spontaneous speech.

3. You are Mr. Davis's new speech writer. He has handed you Speech 1 with orders to make it "snappier". You interpret this to mean that it should be closer to spontaneous speech. Rewrite the speech.

4. You are Mr. Wright's speech writer. He has just told you to do a more serious job on your draft of Speech 2. Rewrite the text.

WRITTEN MODES: WRITTEN TO BE SPOKEN
AS IF NOT WRITTEN, AND WRITTEN TO BE READ

The following page from a TV shooting script of Harold Pinter's play *The Basement*, displays two modes. The speeches by the characters Law and Stott are written to be spoken as if not written. Everything else on the page is written to be read.

EXERCISE:

What kind of spontaneous speech does Law's first passage imitate — monologing or conversing? Give markers.

EXERCISE:

Show how the non dialogue portions of the TV script are marked for the mode written to be read.

Although the typed portions and the additions written in by hand are in the same mode, they are not completely similar. To see the difference, try reading the text aloud. (①/₆ ✱ would be spoken "one circled, followed by sixteen a bit below followed by an asterisk".) This is as much a discussion of the symbols as it is a translation of them to the spoken mode.

~~INTERIOR ROOM.~~
~~THE ROOM.~~

~~INTERIOR BATHROOM.~~

LAW IN BATHROOM, AT THE
AIRING CUPBOARD. HE SWIFTLY
THROWS ASIDE A NUMBER OF
TOWELS, CHOOSES A SOFT ONE
WITH A FLORAL PATTERN.

~~INTERIOR ROOM.~~

② 36 LAW COMES IN WITH A TOWEL.

MS over Gerry at Joe into T2s over Gerry. hold on Joe when Gerry leaves frame.

LAW: Here's a towel. Go on,

give it a good wipe. / That's it.

You didn't walk here, did you?

You're soaking. What happened to

your car? You could have driven

here. Why didn't you give me a

ring? But how did you know my

address? My God, it's years. If

you'd have rung I would have picked

you up. I would have picked you up

in my car. What happened to your

car?

INSERT

① 15 *CU Gerry wiping for intercuts hold for Gerry's line.*

STOTT FINISHES DRYING HIS
HAIR, PUTS THE TOWEL ON THE
ARM OF A CHAIR.

STOTT: I got rid of it.

LAW: But how are you? Are you

well? You look well.

① 16 * *W2S towards fire place.*
    hold as master until Joe goes for drink.
② 17 MS JOE
① 18 MS GERRY
② 19 MS JOE
① 20 MS GERRY

WRITTEN MODE: WRITTEN TO BE READ

The "Aerofin" directions, especially the table, are written to be read.

EXERCISE:

The plumber installing an "Aerofin" system in your summer cottage 200 miles away has left the instructions behind. You are about to telephone him the information, and, in order to avoid confusion, are writing out the table in a form which can be read over the telephone. Produce the first hundred words of this script, and comment on the differences between the mode "written to be spoken", which is what you will produce, and "written to be read", which is the form in which it is printed here.

AEROFIN

PIPING—FLEXITUBE

PIPING CONNECTIONS — IMPORTANT NOTES

1. In Diagrams 1 and 9 note Dimensions from Heater "run out" to check Valve, Thermostatic Air Trap Branch (if any) and Return Manifold. Use Check Valves with Flappers hanging only 15 deg. from vertical.

2. Note Size of Air Vent Lines to which Thermostatic Traps are attached. These Lines must be properly pitched, so that no "pockets" exist that could prevent the free venting of air. All Valves and Traps are to be located outside the casing.

3. The Drip from the Steam Main must be on the Pressure Side of the *Aerofin* Control Valve, and Drip connected as per Diagrams, thru cooling leg and Thermostatic Trap, then into main Return Line beyond the Float Trap handling the condensation from the *Aerofin* itself. Avoid dripping Steam Mains into the *Aerofin* Units themselves.

4. If an Open Circuit Gravity System is used on Low Pressure Boilers and the Return from *Aerofin* is connected to such Boilers below the Water Line, the *Aerofin* must be placed at a sufficient distance above the Water Line of the Boiler so that the maximum Pressure cannot flood the Heaters. (If pump and receiver or Boiler Return Trap are used for return of condensate to Boiler this provision may be ignored.)

5. Wherever a Control Valve is placed on any individual Heater or group of Heaters, such individual Heater or group of Heaters must have a separate Float Trap with individual Air Lines on Return Connection, making this Heater or group of Heaters, so controlled, an Independent Unit. This is illustrated in Diagram 5.

6. With the Closed Circuit Gravity Return to Boiler, the bottom of the *Aerofin* must be not less than 30 in. above Water Line of boiler. Thermostatic Control cannot be used on the Steam Supply Lines.

7. For *Flexitube Aerofin* Units installed with Horizontal Tubes (Horizontal Air Flow), the Units should be set with a pitch toward the Drip Header of not less than ½ in. for Units up to 6 ft. 0 in. in length—and 1 in. for Units over 6 ft. in length of Tubes. For *Flexitube Aerofin* Units installed flat (Vertical Air Flow) set and pitch Units in accordance with Diagram 4.

8. Steam Mains, Return Mains and Risers should be anchored and supported independent of *Aerofin* Units.

9. Steam Mains and Branches to *Aerofin* should be installed with ample provision for expansion and contraction.

10. Dirt pocket, if desired, should be installed in vertical return leg between heater and swing check valve and should be at least 6 inches deep.

•

SIZES OF SUPPLY AND RETURN MAINS

Based on: 6000 ft. per Minute Velocity of Steam

100 ft. Length of Run

Pounds of Steam Condensed per Hour	5 Lbs. Steam Pressure			50 Lbs. Steam Pressure		
	Size of Supply Inches	Size of Gravity Return Inches	Size of Vacuum Return Inches	Size of Supply Inches	Size of Return to Trap Inches	Open Return Beyond Trap Inches
200	1½	1¼	¾	1	¾	1¼
400	2	1¼	¾	1¼	1	1¼
600	2½	1½	1	1½	1¼	1½
800	3	2	1¼	2	1½	2
1000	3½	2	1¼	2	1½	2
1200	3½	2	1¼	2	1½	2
1600	4	2½	1½	2½	2	2½
2200	5	3	2	3	2	3
2600	5	3	2	3	2½	3
3200	6	3½	2½	3½	2½	3½
3600	6	3½	2½	3½	2½	3½
4200	7	4	3	4	3	4
4800	7	4	3	4	3	4
6500	8	4	3½	5	3	4
8000	9	5	3½	5	3½	5
9000	10	5	4	6	3½	5
10000	10	5	4	6	3½	5
14000	12	6	5	7	4	6

[19]

WRITTEN MODE: WRITTEN TO BE READ AS SPEECH

There are two modes in this passage from Hemingway's novel — written to be read and written to be read as speech.

EXERCISE:

Compare the passages of dialogue in the novel with the transcription of children speaking on page 84. What features of spontaneous speech has Hemingway imitated? How does the imitation differ from the real thing?

---

62   THE SUN ALSO RISES

"Yes, sir."

"What is the oldest brandy you have?"

"Eighteen eleven, sir."

"Bring us a bottle."

"I say. Don't be ostentatious. Call him off, Jake." 5

"Listen, my dear. I get more value for my money in old brandy than in any other antiquities."

"Got many antiquities?"

"I got a houseful." 10

Finally we went up to Montmartre. Inside Zelli's it was crowded, smoky, and noisy. The music hit you as you went in. Brett and I danced. It was so crowded we could barely move. The nigger drummer waved at Brett. We were caught in the jam, dancing in one place in front of him.

"Hahre you?" 15

"Great."

"Thaats good."

He was all teeth and lips.

"He's a great friend of mine," Brett said. "Damn good drummer." 20

The music stopped and we started toward the table where the count sat. Then the music started again and we danced. I looked at the count. He was sitting at the table smoking a cigar. The music stopped again. 25

"Let's go over."

Brett started toward the table. The music started and again we danced, tight in the crowd.

"You are a rotten dancer, Jake. Michael's the best dancer I know." 30

"He's splendid."

"He's got his points."

"I like him," I said. "I'm damned fond of him."

WRITTEN MODE: WRITTEN TO BE READ AS THOUGHT

Although much of this text (from James Joyce's novel *Ulysses*) is written to be read and written to be read as speech, it includes language which attempts to imitate spontaneous thinking.

The major clause sentence, ''the coals were reddening'' is marked, by its minor clause structure and by the narrative tag ''he said'', as written to be read as speech.

Leopold Bloom ate with relish the inner organs of beasts and fowls. He liked thick giblet soup, nutty gizzards, a stuffed roast heart, liver slices fried with crustcrumbs, fried hencod's roes. Most of all he liked grilled mutton kidneys which gave to his palate a fine tang of faintly scented urine. 5

Kidneys were in his mind as he moved about the kitchen softly, righting her breakfast things on the humpy tray. Gelid light and air were in the kitchen but out of doors gentle summer morning everywhere. Made him feel a bit peckish.

The coals were reddening. 10

Another slice of bread and butter: three, four: right. She didn't like her plate full. Right. He turned from the tray, lifted the kettle off the hob and set it sideways on the fire. It sat there, dull and squat, its spout stuck out. Cup of tea soon. Good. Mouth dry. The cat walked stiffly round a leg of the table with tail on high. 15

—Mkgnao!

—O, there you are, Mr Bloom said, turning from the fire.

The cat mewed in answer and stalked again stiffly round a leg of the table, mewing. Just how she stalks over my writing-table. Prr. Scratch my head. Prr. 20

Mr Bloom watched curiously, kindly, the lithe black form. Clean to see: the gloss of her sleek hide, the white button under the butt of her tail, the green flashing eyes. He bent down to her, his hands on his knees.

—Milk for the pussens, he said. 25

—Mrkgnao! the cat cried.

They call them stupid. They understand what we say better than we understand them. She understands all she wants to. Vindictive too. Wonder what I look like to her. Height of a tower? No, she can jump me. 30

—Afraid of the chickens she is, he said mockingly. Afraid of the chookchooks. I never saw such a stupid pussens as the pussens.

Cruel. Her nature. Curious mice never squeal. Seem to like it. 35

—Mrkgnao! the cat said loudly.

She blinked up out of her avid shameclosing eyes, mewing plaintively and long, showing him her milkwhite teeth. He watched the dark eyeslits narrowing with greed till her eyes were green stones. Then he went to the dresser, took the jug 40

[55]

When the text shifts from a major clause ''It sat there, dull and squat, its spout stuck out'' to a series of minor clauses, ''Cup of tea soon. Good. Mouth dry.'' and then back to a major clause ''the cat walked stiffly round a leg of the table with tail on high'', the reader senses immediately a change in mode. We have been ''listening'' to Mr Bloom think.

One of the clues to this modality is the relationship of lexical items in the minor clauses to objects which are set forth by the narrative portions as part of the thinker's environment. Food, for instance, as a part of Bloom's environment, prepares us to accept ''mouth dry'' as one of his thoughts.

EXERCISE:

Comment fully on any one of the passages imitating Bloom's spontaneous thought.

WRITTEN MODE: WRITTEN TO BE READ

Although the following business memoranda are written to be read, they differ in a way characteristic of spoken language: the first could be called written conversing and the second written monologuing.

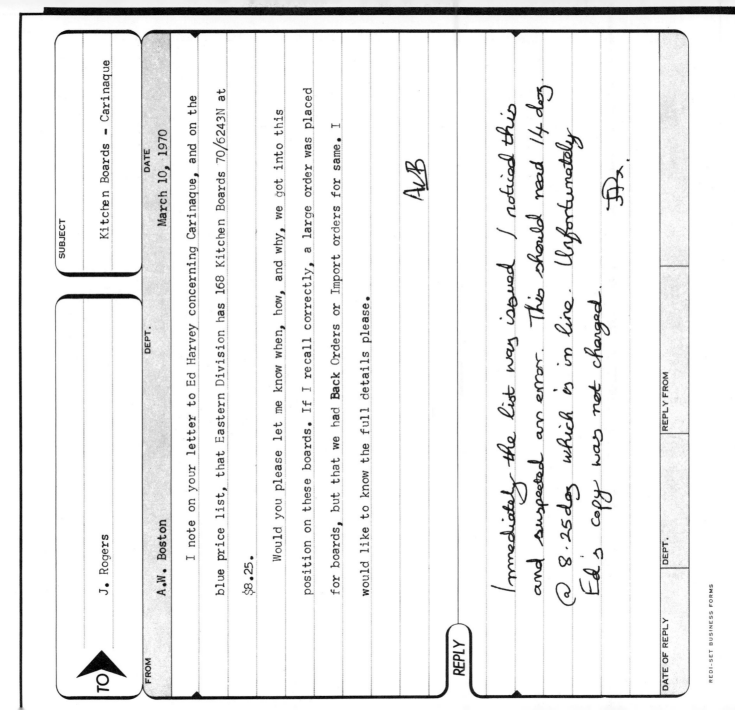

TO		SUBJECT
J. Rogers		Kitchen Boards — Carinaque

FROM	DEPT.	DATE
A.W. Boston		March 10, 1970

I note on your letter to Ed Harvey concerning Carinaque, and on the blue price list, that Eastern Division has 168 Kitchen Boards 70/6243N at $8.25.

Would you please let me know when, how, and why, we got into this position on these boards. If I recall correctly, a large order was placed for boards, but that we had **Back** Orders or Import orders for same. I would like to know the full details please.

AWB

REPLY

Immediately the list was issued I noticed this and suspected an error. This should read 14 days @ 8.25 dos which is in line. Unfortunately Ed's copy was not changed.

JR.

DATE OF REPLY	DEPT.	REPLY FROM

REDI-SET BUSINESS FORMS

SUBJECT

Weekly Summary of Shipments,

Inventories and Purchases —

Sept. 18th

TO

J. Rogers & R.B. Warner

DEPT. ___

DATE September 28, 1970

I note some improvement in the inventory position in Eastern

Division, and on the September 18th Weekly Summary of Shipments, Inventories

and Purchases, the inventory was being reduced by some $60,000.

This is a good step in the right direction, and I trust that "R"

Department sales will catch the purchases to alleviate the problem in that

Department by the end of the month.

I am glad to see that "C" Department has finally come down, and

that "B" Department is coming back into shape.

AWB

FROM

A.W. Boston

DEPT. ___

REPLY

DATE OF REPLY | **DEPT.** | **REPLY FROM**

REDI-SET BUSINESS FORMS

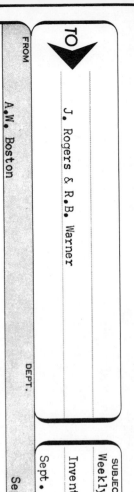

EXERCISES:

1. Show how the memos are marked for conversation and monologue in a way similar to spoken language.

2. Show markers of written conversing which are not characteristic of spoken language.

PERSONAL TENOR

The formality or informality of the social relation between a speaker and his audience influences his language. Suppose a man has one purposive role — the desire to talk about nuclear physics — and a constant desire to teach that particular field of discourse. The formality of the situations in which he can teach nuclear physics will vary considerably. He may be chatting with several students in a bar. Given this social situation, the personal tenor will, in all probability, be fairly informal. On the other hand, he may be dressed in the traditional blue suit, standing in splendid isolation on a platform behind an imposing podium, and lecturing to a large class. Given this social situation, the personal tenor will, in all probability, be quite formal.

The relationship between personal tenor and situation is mutual: not only does the situation influence the language patterns; the language patterns can change the situation. The physics instructor, suddenly noticing that the students at his lecture are falling asleep, can step out from behind his podium and pursue a point through informal conversation with his audience.

Personal tenor does not offer a choice of one or the other — formal or informal. Rather it offers a range from the highly formal to the very informal. Most language is neither at one end nor at the other, but somewhere comfortably in the middle.

INFORMAL

This is a friendly letter, the personal tenor of which, as one would expect, is informal. The informality is indicated by the grammar, lexis, and graphology of the letter.

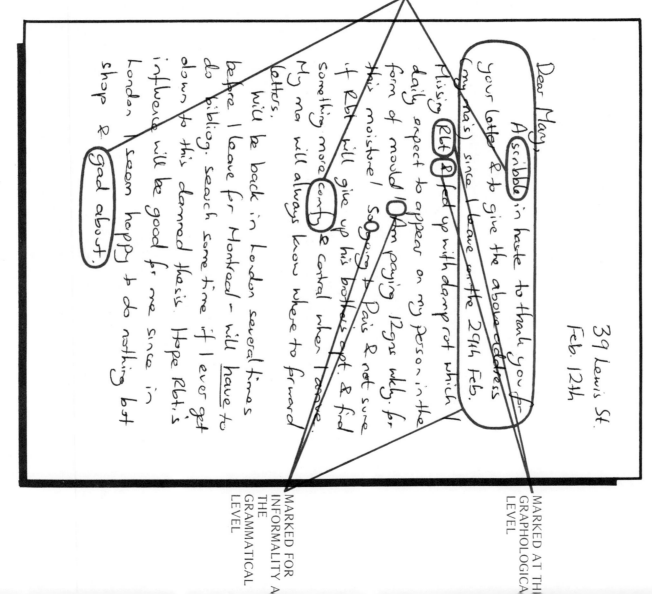

MARKED AT THE LEXICAL LEVEL

MARKED AT THE GRAPHOLOGICAL LEVEL

MARKED FOR INFORMALITY AT THE GRAPHOLOGICAL LEVEL

MARKED FOR INFORMALITY AT THE GRAMMATICAL LEVEL

39 Lewis St.
Feb. 12th

Dear May,

A scribble in haste to thank you for your letter & to give the above address (my ma's) since I leave on the 29th Feb.

Pleasing RLt fed up with damp rot which I daily expect to appear on my person in the form of mould! Am paying 12gns wkly. for this moisture! So going to Paris & not sure if RLt will give up his brother's apt. & find something more comfy. & central when I arrive.

My ma will always know where to forward letters.

Will be back in London several times before I leave for Montreal — will have to do bibliog. search some time if I ever get down to this damned thesis. Hope RLt's influence will be good for me since in London I seem happy & do nothing but shop & gad about.

EXERCISES:

1. Identify additional markers of informality at each of the three levels (lexical, grammatical, and graphological).

2. By changing these markers, produce a letter with a more formal personal tenor.

FORMAL

This sample wedding invitation, from a manual used by a Canadian engraving company, is highly formal.

WEDDING INVITATIONS

ISSUED BY PARENTS

Mr. and Mrs. Lewis Phillips Edmondson

request the honour of your presence

at the marriage of their daughter

Marilyn Louise

to

Mr. Bradley Howard Williamson, junior

on Thursday, the twelfth of June

Nineteen hundred and fifty-eight

at eight o'clock

Saint Stephen's Episcopal Church

Atlanta, Georgia

The date line may also be engraved, "Thursday evening, the twelfth of June."

The year line may be omitted, or it may read: "One thousand nine hundred and fifty-eight." Capitalization of the first word in the year line is usually employed when the use of a lower-case letter would otherwise show several successive lines beginning with a lower-case letter. Any engraver familiar with good styling can suggest whether a capital or lower-case letter seems appropriate.

[28]

FORMAL

A preface to a scholarly work may have an almost ceremonial status. This results in formal — and, in some cases, stilted — language. Grammatical and lexical formality can best be seen by looking at less formal alternatives. Consider the following sentences as alternative openings for paragraphs 3, 4, and 5:

"It's arranged like the earlier catalogues";

"It cost so much to print that the trustees couldn't pay for it";

"Miss Johnson capably edited the catalogue, and we are indebted to her for giving our readers this essential tool."

EXERCISES:

1. In "Preface" (below), comment on the attention paid to graphological usage.

2. Replace the circled lexical items with less formal equivalents.

Preface

1 The following catalogue lists the books in Dr. Williams's Library published from 1900 to 1950 (inclusive.) With the exception of works in certain series all books published before 1900, even though added to the Library since that date, have been (excluded.)

2 The catalogue (supersedes) the *Catalogue of additions in the years 1900–1921*, the *Catalogue of additions in the years 1922–1932* and the accession lists printed in the Library Bulletins from 1933 to 1951.*

3 In (arrangement) the plan of earlier catalogues has been followed. The first part is an author catalogue. The second part, or Supplement, is a list of periodicals and serials. Books published in continuous series regularly taken in the Library are listed in the Supplement, but complete author references to all entries in the Supplement are included in the author catalogue.

4 The cost of printing the Catalogue was so great that the Trustees were unable to finance it from their own resources. For its production they are indebted to the following Charitable Trusts for generous support: The Aston Charities Trust, The Goldsmiths' Company, The Sir Halley Stewart Trust, and The Wallace Alfred Smith Trust, and to several other Trusts which wish to remain anonymous. The Trustees take this opportunity of (recording their gratitude) to these Bodies, as also to the many readers of the Library who have (annually) contributed towards the cost of the work through the Friends of Dr. Williams's Library since the formation of that Society in 1946.

5 The work of editing the Catalogue has been in the capable hands of Miss D. M. Johnson, to whom the Library is indebted for the production of a work which will be an essential tool for the Library's regular readers; and, it is hoped, a useful work of reference to many others interested in the literature of theology, philosophy and related subjects during the present century.

15th November, 1954.

* It supersedes the earlier catalogues mentioned except in so far as these contain entries for works published before 1900.

MIXED FORMAL/INFORMAL

In this letter, the writer is playing two roles, friend and business-man. "John" informally closes the letter to a friend, while the "Yours sincerely" which immediately follows conforms to the formal pattern of a business latter.

Dear John,

I thought it best to write you privately in regard
to your complaint over the way Continental Express handled
the transport of your trunk to Toronto. Needless to say
I do not think it justified, but there is some explanation   5
due to you.

I would say that it was only on Thursday the 1st inst.,
that Roger gave me your address hence the delay in my writing
to you.

As you know the actual despatch of your trunk was handled   10
by our London Office this being usual for overseas shipments.
After one unfortunate experience some time ago when our
London Office sent documents to a consignee it is the practice
to use a Broker. Goods were not collected at Docks and
warehousing charges far exceeded the 10 Dollars which is the   15
basic Broker's charge. I agree that in your case you wanted
your trunk without delay so that without a doubt you made
contact immediately on your arrival in Toronto. However, in
accordance with the now uniform practice our London Office
sent the documents to their Broker. The basic fee of 10 Dollars   20
is rather high for U.K. standards but apparently in Canada this
is normal.

I did expect all charges to be debited to us at Brighton
and this I told you before departure, but the cost would have
been the same, and our London Office could not arrange this   25
anyway! I enclose a receipt for the twelve pounds paid to us,
just in case you should require it.

I hope you are keeping well and enjoying your work at
the University. Ray is working hard to build up his church
at Corley Park and is finding much success. Martha has   30
improved considerably in health and now she is more or less
fit.

With all good wishes, John.

                    Yours sincerely,

EXERCISE:

This is basically a formal business letter. Describe those places in which an informal personal tenor intrudes.

FUNCTIONAL TENOR

Functional tenor is the organization of those patterns, within language, which are related to the social intention of the speaker. "Good morning", spoken cheerfully to one's neighbour, is the result of a desire to convey good will. The conveyance of significant weather information is minimal. As a greeting, "good morning" works even when it's cold and raining. A marine weather forecast, on the other hand, must convey technical information, and convey it accurately. The social intention of the marine weather forecaster is to inform.

These functional tenors, *phatic communion* in the greeting and *expository* in the forecast, are only two among a large number. A person may wish to do more than simply present information; he may actively want others to learn it. The language in this case is marked for the functional tenor *didactic*.

The range of functional tenors can be seen if we imagine a concrete situation — a library which ought to be a quiet place — and think of the possible number of responses to persistent giggling in one corner.

The remark by one person to another as they walked through the library, "Gee! it's noisy in here, isn't it?", would be *phatic communion*.

The librarian's admonition, "If you continue to giggle like that you will disturb the other readers", would be *persuasion*.

A direct "Be quiet" would be *command*.

An annoyed student's "Hey, shut up!" would be partly *command* and partly *hostility*.

A notice prominently placed at the entrance of the reading room stating "Please note: There is a Lounge in the lower level for the benefit of those who wish to converse" would be *didactic*.

An objective account, prepared by a researcher on student behaviour, of the number of decibels to which giggling must rise before serious students will begin to read less effectively, would probably take the form *expository*.

Functional tenors do not necessarily occur in the pure forms implied by the library examples. A speaker may have several social intentions at the same time, and the description of his functional tenor will therefore be complex. For example, a text dealing with the operation of a lawn mower will be largely *didactic*, but might well include the *command* "Keep your hands away from the blade at all times!" In this case, the text would be marked by a dominant functional tenor, *didactic*, with the subtenor of *command*.

A text might show a more or less equal distribution of functional tenors, as in the treasurer's report (to a small informal club) which seeks to present accurately the financial condition of the club, and is therefore *expository*, but seeks also to amuse the group to whom the report is delivered, and is therefore *entertaining*.

An overt/covert relationship between functional tenors frequently occurs. Many spot commercials on TV for patent medicines describe an impressive list of technical-sounding ingredients. The *overt* functional tenor is *expository*, but the advertisers are obviously more interested in turning their audience into customers than into chemists. Their *covert* functional tenor is *persuasion*.

In the rest of this section you will find two series of texts marked for functional tenor.

1. The first series consists of four uncomplicated texts clearly marked for the functional tenors phatic communion, expository, persuasion, and didactic.

2. The second series has twelve complex texts which are still strongly marked for a single functional tenor.

PHATIC COMMUNION

This Father's Day card has a number of features which serve one purpose — that of generating a feeling of good will. Although the card is mass produced, its grammar, lexis, and graphology suggest a personal relationship between speaker and addressee. The nonverbal equivalent of this card would be a hug.

GRAPHOLOGICAL MARKERS
(the imitation of handwriting)

GRAMMATICAL MARKERS

LEXICAL MARKERS

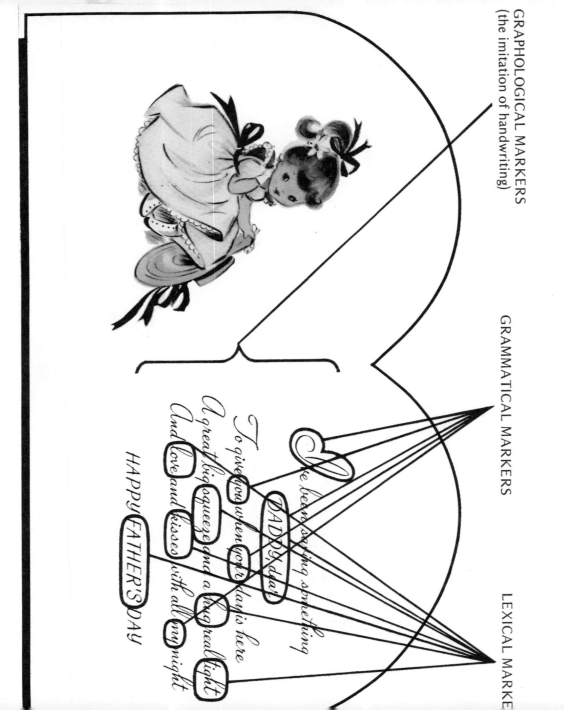

The best way of saying something
To give you when your day is here
DADDY dear,
A great big squeeze and a great big hug
And love and kisses with all my might

HAPPY FATHER'S DAY

EXPOSITORY

The functional tenor of "Export A" is expository. The field of discourse, cigarettes, is firmly established, but, except for the word "finest" there is, at the level of lexis, nothing which indicates an *attitude* towards that field.

The persuasive devices of this advertisement are features other than language: the bold print emphasizes the brand name, the script suggests elegance, and the picture adds charm.

The desire to sell is reflected much more directly in the language of "Peter Dawson" than in that of "Export A".

Try to construct a situation to fit the handwritten note. Is it directed to a "best man"? Did Peter Dawson write the note? When looked at closely, the text is, at best, ambiguous. In this instance, clarity is not at all necessary; in fact, its absence helps to emphasize the highly-marked functional tenor of persuasion. In a mere nine words, the handwritten message manages to include not only "best", "deserves", and "best", but also the brand name of the product.

GOOD TO YOUR TASTE. GOOD TO YOUR PURSE.

DIDACTIC

This text lacks the markers of persuasion which are present in Peter Dawson. The functional tenor appears to be expository: the few markers of praise ("international repute" and "enjoyed") are more than balanced by the objective tone in which the drinks are described.

The text goes *beyond* the merely expository in its obvious attempt to help the reader learn. The three parallel adjuncts, with their carefully organized offering of alternatives, are grammatical markers of didactic functional tenor. Note how the use of graphic resources helps to establish the functional tenor.

The most interesting feature is the rather formal sentence "Dubonnet is enjoyed . . . ." Perhaps the European atmosphere of the advertisement explains the use of a passive construction, rather than a "crude" imperative.

This passage from James Joyce's novel *A Portrait of the Artist as a Young Man* describes the type of situation in which phatic communion takes place, and provides examples of its occurrence.

3 o   *A Portrait of the Artist*

Why did Mr Barrett in Clongowes call his pandybat a turkey? But Clongowes was far away: and the warm heavy smell of turkey and ham and celery rose from the plates and dishes and the great fire was banked high and red in the grate and the green ivy and red holly made you feel so happy and when dinner was ended the big plumpudding would be carried in, studded with peeled almonds and sprigs of holly, with bluish fire running around it and a little green flag flying from the top.   10

It was his first Christmas dinner and he thought of his little brothers and sisters who were waiting in the nursery, as he had often waited, till the pudding came. The deep low collar and the Eton jacket made him feel queer and oldish: and that morning when his mother had brought him down to the parlour, dressed for mass, his father had cried. That was because he was thinking of his own father. And uncle Charles had said so too.   15

Mr Dedalus covered the dish and began to eat hungrily. Then he said:

—Poor old Christy, he's nearly lopsided now with roguery.   20

—Simon, said Mrs Dedalus, you haven't given Mrs Riordan any sauce.

Mr Dedalus seized the sauceboat.

—Haven't I? he cried. Mrs Riordan, pity the poor blind.   25

Dante covered her plate with her hands and said:

—No, thanks.

Mr Dedalus turned to uncle Charles.

—How are you off, sir?

—Right as the mail, Simon.   30

—You, John?

—I'm all right. Go on yourself.

—Mary? Here, Stephen, here's something to make your hair curl.

He poured sauce freely over Stephen's plate and set the   35 boat again on the table. Then he asked uncle Charles was it tender. Uncle Charles could not speak because his mouth was full but he nodded that it was.

Rank the circled examples in a scale, from those that do nothing more than establish fellowship to those with another purpose. (There is no one correct order for the list.)

EXPOSITORY

"Attraction And Mating", which describes insect behaviour, and summarizes research on the subject, lacks markers of functional tenors such as persuasion, praise, or didacticism. However, the overt markers of hesitation, qualification, and neutrality establish its functional tenor as expository.

Since this is a purely expository text, a background against which other functional tenors will stand out sharply, we have included the entire section "Attraction And Mating".

selection; therefore, many works have not even been mentioned which do in fact contribute information pertinent to this chapter. This chapter also generally omits citation of those papers already summarized in Ribbands' book on the assumption that copies of this book are generally available to all concerned.

ATTRACTION AND MATING

Replacement of a lost or failing queen (supersedure) and production of queens prior to the issue of a swarm appear to involve similar signals. The differences in communication during these two processes will be treated later. In either case, within ten days after the first queen emerges and disposes of her rivals in the colony, she is ready for a mating flight. Exactly when this occurs depends largely upon weather conditions, but prior to the actual mating flight she may make several short orientation flights and thereby learn the position of the colony. The distinctive hive odor and landmarks which figure so prominently in the orientation of bees to their particular colony are possibly learned on these orientation flights. Taber (1954), however, reports that 40 per cent of queens studied left directly on mating flights without having made prior orientation flights.

On the afternoon of the mating flight, general hive activity rises to a higher pitch than normal, and just before the queen leaves the hive, one can notice the workers throughout the colony milling about. Aggressive behavior and special feeding of the queen by workers reportedly precede queen departure (Allen, 1956; Hammann, 1957; Ruttner, 1957). Eventually, what resembles a small swarm leaves the hive via its entrance; the queen then leaves this group and flies off by herself. Within one-half to one hour she returns, generally with a "mating sign" still attached to the tip of her abdomen. Although she may have

5

10

15

20

EXERCISE:

Show the means by which the objectivity of this text is maintained.

mated enough on this one flight to have a lifetime supply of sperm, queens usually take several mating flights before laying (Alber et al., 1955; Woyke and Ruttner, 1958).

What transpires during this queen flight is a difficult problem to study, since mating apparently occurs too high to be seen. Although there is by no means universal agreement on this point, certain sites appear to be drone congregation areas which queens eventually reach on their mating flights (see Zmarlicki and Morse, 1963; Butler and Fairey, 1964; and Ruttner and Ruttner, 1965). Some of these areas seem to be remarkably stable and persist in the same location for several successive years. A clearing, low hilltop, or some secluded spot free from high winds may function in such a capacity, but the precise requirements for such an area are not yet known.

Once one has seen such an area, however, he can have little doubt that drone congregation areas exist. The sound of thousands of drones just out of sight overhead (with the aid of binoculars they can be seen cruising about, once a general sound source has been located) resembles that of a swarm of bees in flight, but there is no precise center to this sound. Drones in these groups apparently come from several hives in the area. Small birds, dragonflies, and butterflies in the area are very likely to be pursued by a number of drones if they venture too high. Similarly, a stick or stone thrown high into the air results in a "comet" of drones pursuing the object until it hits the ground. Sometimes the drones even go into the grass as a result of their intense pursuit of an object and can be caught with a net. Ruttner and Ruttner (1965) investigated several of these areas over a period of time. They found that a queen tethered to a gas-filled balloon failed to attract drones when moved beyond a certain point with respect to the apparent center of the congregation area.

It would appear, then, that it is no longer a question of whether such congregations exist, but rather it is a problem of determining the factors responsible for such mating aggregations. Conceivably, a circular flight pattern by a virgin queen could result in a number of drones heading upwind and congregating about her—attraction of drones to queens tethered to balloons regardless of the location in which this was attempted supports this possibility (Butler and Fairey, 1964). Alternatively, especially in areas with varied topography, drones could be attracted to distinctive geographic sites—persistence of congregations for several weeks or under similar conditions in different years supports this notion. In the latter case, queens could be attracted either by the drone congregation itself or to the same site for the same reasons as the drones.

Formation of a mating aggregation has special advantages in increasing the probability of queens being found by drones and in providing some protection against predators. That is, predators would be unlikely to find a queen among the thousands of flying drones present in the same locality.

The factors responsible for mating aggregations relate to the mating activity which follows. Butler and Fairey (1964) suggest that drones get within sight of queens largely by utilizing odor stimuli from downwind and then employ visual cues during the final act of mating. The work of Gary (1963), together with my own observations of drone behavior in drone aggregations, however, reveals that a "comet" of drones forms about any moving object, even about other drones. If the proper chemicals are present on the moving object, more drones stay with the object longer and attempt to mount it. Gary also found that tactile stimuli may be involved, since mating did not proceed to completion unless the queen's sting chamber was open.

Many investigators have attempted to find the chemical or chemicals responsible for attracting drones to queens during the mating flight. Fractions obtained from the head, thorax, or abdomen all attract drones when raised high into the air on filter paper, but the head fraction is by far the most attractive (Gary, 1962; Pain and Ruttner, 1963). At least one secretion of the mandibular glands, 9-ketodec-2-trans-enoic acid, is strongly attractive to drones, but it is not necessarily the sole factor responsible for initiating copulation. Successful mating by queens which have had their mandibular glands removed rules out this source of queen substance as necessary for successful mating (Morse et al., 1962). Renner and Baumann (1964) also report subepidermal cells located in the dorsal region of the queen's abdomen, which appear glandular in nature. The odor from these glands is apparently very strong in young virgin queens and could function during attraction of drones to queens. Conceivably, one chemical could serve in attracting drones from a distance, visual cues could orient the drone into position behind a fast-moving queen, and another odor (or odors) could result in a final copulation attempt. Alternatively, some other combination of these events might be involved.

Evidence (Gary, 1963) indicates that drones normally approach a queen from behind and below and then assume a dorsal position during mating. As the drone's genitalia move into the sting chamber, tracheal air sac pressure from within the drone leads to an eversion of his genitalia, a slight explosion, and a resultant separation of the paralyzed drone from the queen. The queen can repeat this procedure within seconds, mate with up to ten different drones on a mating flight (reviewed by Ruttner, 1964), and return to the hive with a lifetime supply of sperm.

Certain questions in view of the evidence above now become well defined in connection with the attraction and mating of bees. We must still determine the parameters that define a drone congregation area. When the necessary signals are understood, we should be able to create such aggregations artificially in certain locations. We must also determine which pheromone or combination of pheromones and visual signals is responsible for copulatory activity. Likewise, we need to determine the stimulus responsible for the opening of a queen's sting chamber at the actual time of mating. Other, less well-defined questions need further study. Among these are a determination of which signals stimulate a queen to leave the hive on her mating flight and whether drone congregation areas are necessary for queen mating. 120

COLONY ORGANIZATION

Queen Influence on Workers

A queen both directly and indirectly influences workers in the colony. The direct influences include all those signals produced by a queen which are immediately perceived by workers and which regulate the attitude of workers toward each other and toward the queen. The indirect influence is much more difficult to study and includes such factors as the number of eggs laid relative to available space, ratio of drone to worker eggs laid, and ratio of eggs laid to the available supply of adult workers. One would suspect that these indirect influences, which will be treated only incidentally in this account, are integral parts of cybernetic systems. 125

A colony must have a queen or be in the process of producing a queen if it is to survive long. As a laying queen moves over the combs, she is constantly surrounded by a "retinue" of workers who touch and lick her body. Obviously she maintains a certain attractiveness to workers in the colony, and workers show signs of queenlessness within a few hours after losing her. A few days after such a loss, queen cell building will begin, and some of the workers will exhibit enlarged ovaries. 140

If a queen is restrained in a wire-screen cage in her colony, workers continue many of their activities as if they still had a queen, and apparently they show no enlargement of ovaries (Verheijen-Voogd, 1959). On the basis of this and other reports in the literature, one might classify signals produced as a result of queen presence and which influence workers as (1) inhibition of queen cell building, (2) inhibition of ovary development, and (3) attraction of workers. These can function by worker reception of an odor emanating from some 145

EXPOSITORY

The language of this page from a university calendar is highly marked as functional tenor expository. The material is carefully organized. The title, "Admission to the University", indicates the field of discourse, a sub-title indicates the subfield, and numbered subheadings indicate sub-subfields.

Consider the functional tenors the author might have used. Section One might have begun negatively, with an overt, forbidding command: "Do not apply for admission unless you have standing in four acceptable subjects", et cetera. Or, it might have had a warmly encouraging opening. "Our University welcomes Ontario Grade XIII students who have standing in four acceptable subjects", et cetera. In almost no case, however, has the text departed from expository prose.

Admission to the University

REQUIREMENTS FOR ADMISSION IN SEPTEMBER 1969 AND SEPTEMBER 1970

1. GENERAL INFORMATION

Applicants for admission to the University are required to present the Ontario Grade 13 certificate with standing in at least four acceptable subjects (seven credits) and with a minimum overall average of 60.0%. Certificates equivalent to Ontario Grade 13 are listed in Section 7.

Candidates who have required more than two years in the final two grades of high school to obtain the admission requirements normally must have a Grade 13 average of at least 65.0%.

In assessing a candidate for admission the University considers the overall academic record, the confidential report of the high school, and all available results of Scholastic Aptitude and Achievement Tests.

Candidates are advised that the holding of the published admission requirements means only that they are eligible for selection.

2. GRADE 13 REQUIREMENTS

Candidates for a Bachelor of Arts degree in the Faculty of Arts and Science are required to present at least four acceptable subjects, comprising at least seven credits with a minimum overall average of 60.0%.

3. ACCEPTABLE GRADE 13 SUBJECTS

The following Grade 13 (or equivalent) subjects are acceptable:

SUBJECT	CREDITS	SUBJECT	CREDITS
English	2	History	1
Français	2	Mathematics A *and* B (2 subjects)	3
French	2		
Anglais	2	Mathematics A *or* B alone	2
German	2	Physics	1
Greek	2	Chemistry	1
Italian	2	Biology	1
Latin	2	Music	1
Russian	2	Art	1
Spanish	2		
Geography	1		

N.B. Candidates may offer only one of Music or Art.

Ontario applicants may also offer Hebrew by special arrangement. The University will also consider other languages at the intermediate level.

4. SCHOLASTIC APTITUDE TESTS

Candidates for the First Year of a degree programme are required to submit Scholastic Aptitude Test scores.

Candidates attending Canadian high schools must present scores from the Aptitude Tests (both Verbal and Mathematical) offered by The (Canadian) Service for Admission to Colleges and Universities. Information is available at the high schools. Candidates from the United States must present Scholastic Aptitude Test scores (both Verbal and Mathematical) offered by the College Entrance Examination Board. For information write to the College Entrance Examination Board, Box 592, Princeton, New Jersey 08540, U.S.A.

SACU (Can.) and CEEB Achievement Test scores, while not mandatory, are highly recommended.

N.B. Candidates who are applying under the Mature Student regulations (See Sec. 9), and those whose secondary school education was in a language

The Petrie Science Building

EXERCISES:

1. How does the sentence "For information write to the College Entrance Examination Board . . . ." differ grammatically from the rest of the text?

2. Change the functional tenor by rewriting the entire text as a series of direct commands to the reader.

NARRATIVE

Narration forms a special class of expository material, in which the thing described is an event which has happened or is happening. In this selection, from a history book, the order of the presentation is chronological: all main verbs are in the past tense, and any theorizing, for example, the nominal adjunct "who in any case may have hoped to be *tertius gaudens*", is clearly related to an action.

ANGLO-FRENCH ALLIANCE, 1527
317

Milan bound themselves to resist the designs of Charles. The king of England, who was understood to have already given his countenance, was named protector of the new confederation. Despite its high patronage, the league of Cognac accomplished nothing. Francis, anxious to make up for the boredom of his captivity, gave himself up to pleasure and spent his money upon buildings instead of upon armaments; Henry was short of funds, and Wolsey, who in any case may have hoped to be *tertius gaudens*, could not have precipitated England into a war against the Netherlands even had he wished to do so. The pope's Italian allies, after some initial successes, lost heart. Sforza surrendered Milan in July and in September imperialist troops under Moncada supported by cardinal Colonna occupied Rome and hunted the pope into the castle of San Angelo. Henry, in reply to papal appeals, sent the comforting message to the successor of St. Peter[1] *oravi ne deficiat fides tua* along with a promise of 30,000 ducats which, to the gratified astonishment of the cardinals, actually arrived in Rome early in 1527.[2] Wolsey was complimented by his fellow countrymen on having kept England clear of the Italian disasters; but he was in fact meditating a still closer alliance with France, and in March 1527 there arrived in London the bishop of Tarbes who, on 30 April,[3] signed at Westminster treaties uniting Henry and Francis in a perpetual peace and binding them to make war upon Charles as soon as the emperor refused to free the French king's sons and to pay the debts of the king of England. By the terms of this treaty Mary was to marry either Francis himself or his second son, and in order to bring all to perfection Wolsey proposed to go to France in person. Before he set out, however, occurred an event which gave a new justification and a new direction to his policy. On 6 May the imperialist troops, unfed, unpaid, and many of them Lutheran, broke into the Holy City itself. The hard-bitten Georg von Frundsberg had already succumbed to apoplexy as he endeavoured to control his mutinous landsknechts; Bourbon, who was in command, was killed during the assault, and Spaniards and Germans, casting discipline to the winds, gave Rome to a sack whose brutality horrified the civilized world. The pope was again compelled to take refuge in the castle of San Angelo and there he remained

[1] Ibid. iv. ii. 1137.   [2] Ibid. iv. ii. 1278.
[3] Ibid. iv. ii. 1382.

Not all scholarship is as objective as it could be. This text is a description of William of Orange by an author who does not hesitate to blame him.

156 THOMAS KEN: BISHOP AND NON-JUROR

In the public Declaration by which he sought to justify his invasion of England, he appeared, by references to the supposititious birth of a Prince of Wales, to encourage belief in a canard which he must have known to be utterly and basely untrue. If he really believed the ridiculous and malicious "warming-pan" calumny, it is scarcely creditable to his judgement; if, as is almost certain, he disbelieved it, his behaviour in apparently accepting it in order to inflame public opinion against the King is beneath all contempt.

His own personal life, as we have seen, was far from irreproachable, for all his Calvinistic sanctimoniousness. His cold and callous harshness towards his wife, his sordid and joyless adulteries, his calculated political manœuvrings and duplicities, preclude any attempt to present William of Orange as a pure-souled, high-minded, disinterested lover of liberty and true religion.

Yet few men are altogether bad and William had his good points, little calculated though they may have been to inspire affection. Even that stern critic of his character, Dr Johnson, whose views on the Prince are quoted above, was ready to admit that "none ever denied him the resplendent qualities of steady resolution and personal courage".[1] These, indeed, were the very qualities—in combination with his political acumen, lack of scruple, and shrewd judgement of men—which had won for him the glittering prize now firmly in his grasp. They were the qualities most needed now that he found himself the *de facto* ruler of a nation, of which a majority regarded him merely as the lesser of two evils and a considerable minority as an unwanted usurper.

Even with the powerful support of the influential faction which had brought him to England, William soon discovered that his new subjects were no more minded to submit to arbitrary rule on the part of a Dutch Presbyterian Prince than they had been to that of a Papist one. The Convention, in conferring the Crown upon William, had thoughtfully

[1] *Life of Prior.*

EXERCISE:

Attempt to rewrite this page with the studied objectivity of "Attraction And Mating" (pages 111-114).

PERSUASION

Praise and blame are important in this text too, but the main functional tenor, which they help to establish, is persuasion.

EXERCISE:

Discuss how grammar, lexis, mode of discourse and personal tenor contribute to the persuasiveness of this speech.

RECEIVED FEB 19 1971

news

RELEASE: 1 P.M., FEB. 19, 1971

"IL FAUT CULTIVER NOTRE JARDIN"

REMARKS BY HON. STANLEY J. RANDALL
ONTARIO MINISTER OF TRADE AND DEVELOPMENT
TO THE ROTARY CLUB OF TORONTO
ROYAL YORK HOTEL, TORONTO
1 P.M., FRIDAY, FEBRUARY 19, 1971

"WE MUST CULTIVATE OUR GARDEN," WROTE VOLTAIRE OVER 200 YEARS AGO.   5

FOLLOWING THAT SAGE ADVICE, IN MY RECENT SPEECHES
I'VE CONCENTRATED ON HOW TO GET RID OF WEEDS--RADICAL   10
ECONOMIC NATIONALISTS. LIKE WEEDS, ECONOMIC NATIONALISTS
HINDER PRODUCTIVE GROWTH. LIKE WEEDS, THEIR VIRTUES
HAVEN'T BEEN DISCOVERED.

NOW, IT'S ALSO SAID THAT WORK WELL DONE NEVER NEEDS
REDOING--UNLESS, OF COURSE, IT'S WEEDING. SO MY WEEDING   15
WILL CONTINUE.

BUT IN MY REMARKS TODAY I'LL ALSO BE CONCENTRATING

ON WHAT CANADIANS SHOULD BE POSITIVELY PLANTING IN OUR

ECONOMIC GARDEN AND HOW TO MAKE IT GROW HEALTHFULLY.

I'LL BE AS BRIEF AS I CAN, POSITIVE, AND HELPFUL. I

WON'T LEAD YOU DOWN ANY DEAD-END GARDEN PATHS. IN

SHORT: I'LL AVOID THE ECONOMIC NATIONALIST APPROACH,

WHICH HOLDS THAT THE WAY TO GET GRASSROOTS SUPPORT FOR

THEIR CAUSE IS TO SPREAD AROUND A LOT OF FERTILIZER.

* * *

NOW, THE BEST WAY TO WIN AN ARGUMENT IS TO

BEGIN BY BEING RIGHT. IT ALSO HELPS IF YOU HAVE LOGIC,

HISTORY, PERSPECTIVE, AND CONVICTION ON YOUR SIDE.

EVEN MY DETRACTORS WOULD FIND IT HARD TO DENY

THAT JUST 10 YEARS AGO CONVENTIONAL WISDOM HELD THAT

CANADA WAS AN UNDERDEVELOPED COUNTRY...THAT FOREIGN

CAPITAL WAS NEEDED TO SUPPLEMENT DOMESTIC SAVINGS FOR

ECONOMIC GROWTH...AND THAT THE POTENTIAL POLITICAL

IMPLICATIONS WERE NOT SERIOUS, BECAUSE THE MAJOR LENDER

WAS THE U.S., OUR FRIENDLY COUSINS TO THE SOUTH.

TODAY, THE CONVENTIONAL WISDOM PREACHED BY

SOME ECONOMIC NATIONALISTS HOLDS THAT THE U.S. IS A

RACIST AND IMPERIALIST NATION BENT ON SUBVERTING

CANADA BY CONTROLLING ITS ECONOMY...THAT U.S. CORPORATIONS

ARE BEING USED AS THE INSTRUMENTS OF U.S. IMPERIALISM

...AND THAT CANADA IS A DEVELOPED COUNTRY THAT DOESN'T

NEED FOREIGN CAPITAL.

The functional tenor of "Stars might be giants, but film isn't", blame, is strongly marked at the lexical level.

Stars might be giants, but film isn't

120

BLAME

PRAISE

Most bad movies are depressing. But a bad movie like They Might Be Giants, at the Odeon Hyland, Yonge St. at St. Clair, depresses in a specially painful way. A group of gifted people have come together for the seeming purpose of just throwing their talents away.

The film stars George C. Scott, one of America's most powerful imaginative actors. Through a shrewd choice of roles—notably his Oscar—he has achieved a position of esteem such that he can pick and choose his properties.

Scott's co-star is Joanne Woodward, a wonderfully instinctive, often very moving a c t r e s s. Miss Woodward doesn't make all that many films, because, according to her, she wants to pick and choose the roles which she feels are just right for her. (It's also hard to understand why Miss Woodward, an outstandingly b e a u t i f u l woman in person, chooses roles which inevitably end up by having her look as if she'd just been elected Miss Frump of all time).

The film's director, Anthony Harvey, had such a huge success with A Lion in Winter that he, too, would surely have carte blanche to select material which would particularly interest him.

The d r e a d f u l question about this dreadful film, then, is why in the world did these three fine free agents achieve a standstill tie on it? The worst thing about They Might Be Giants is a script by James Goldman, from an unproduced (no wonder!) play of his. Goldman also wrote A Lion in Winter and Harvey must thus have been familiar with his windy rhetoric and fake poetry.

The screenplay for They Might Be Giants is staggeringly bad. Its basic premise is that a highly imaginative paranoid who fancies himself to be Sherlock Holmes is treated by a psychiatrist called Dr. Watson. Scott plays Justin Playfair, an immensely wealthy man with the Holmes delusion, a searcher for truth and integrity.

Miss Woodward plays Dr. Mildred Watson, a psychiatrist who, asked to commit him, instead finds herself greedy brother can have his money, failing under his spell. This is one of those tales in which two misfit, drab people find adventure with one another, and this fatally whimsical Holmes and his Dr. Watson run about New York looking for clues which lead them to a confrontation with the eternal adversary, Dr. Moriarty.

The clues all lead them to encounters with other social drop-outs and eccentrics—a couple who have hidden away in an indoor garden since 1939, a demented young man who thinks he's leading them all in a triumphal parade and informing them that men are all fools, that earth is Eden, and that if God is dead, He laughed Himself to death.

Goldman's unseemly screenplay mixes this kind of blathering pretension with cute, coy eccentric characters (Jack Gilford as a librarian who thinks he's the Scarlet Pimpernel is particularly embarrassing) and a heavily "poetic," symbolic ending which, by trying to mean everything, turns out to mean nothing. Director Harvey permits his leading actors to away at their manner (much the way that Karine Hepburn was urged to caricature herself in A in Winter). Scott plays single note of mad-eyed vor, and Miss Woodward eternally, drably wistful.

They Might Be Giants, even apart from the miserable script and clumsy performances, is a substanfilm on the simplest le The film looks very poprocessed, and the so track is garbled and intinct. Presumably, all people involved thro that they were involthemselves in an off-b meaningful movie, but nice, trashy B-movie w have been much more come.

They Might Be Giants rected by Anthony Har At the Odeon Hyland, Yo St. at St. Clair, 962-2891.

EXERCISE:

Although the functional tenor is clearly blame, there is a lexical set of praise. How do praise and blame interact in this text?

PERSUASION

The examples of the functional tenor persuasion which we have examined so far have been *overt*; that is, they have made no attempt to hide their persuasiveness. Many texts are written to persuade, but in a *covert* way. Such texts generally have one or more clearly marked overt functional tenors. Their markers of persuasion are kept discreetly in the background.

The functional tenor of the text below is not constant. The overall effect is somewhere between expository and didactic. A great deal of information is presented, but the motivating force behind the text is more than the desire to have the reader learn all about "skating".

EXERCISE:

In the text below, what are the markers of the covert functional tenor persuasion?

DUAL 1009SK
PRECISION DESIGN
AND ENGINEERING FEATURES

CONTINUOUSLY VARIABLE, DIRECT-DIAL TRACKING-BALANCE CONTROL™ (Anti-Skating)

What You Should Know About Skating

Skating refers to the side-thrust imparted to the stylus from the offset angle of the tonearm head and the friction between the stylus and the rotating record.

This causes the stylus to "skate" toward the center of the record, thus causing increased force against the inner groove and correspondingly less force against the outer groove. This results in distortion, increased wear on the inner groove and uneven wear on the stylus itself.

Skating is actually not a serious problem with ordinary tonearms, as their bearing friction in the pivot is generally high enough to cancel out or minimize the tendency to skate. Of course, bearing friction high enough to prevent skating is also high enough to compromise tracking performance at the ultra-lightweight forces now made possible by today's finest high compliance cartridges.

Actual Forces Present at Stylus Point

13. K – theoretical force against
tonearm bearing if head
were not angled
Z – direction of force against
tonearm bearing because
of angled head
Sk – skating force
a – angle of offset
head
tonearm
bearing
stylus point

The amount of skating force is directly measurable, and amounts to about 12% of tracking force. Fig. 13 illustrates the physical principle behind skating and the forces that cause it.

A tonearm with 2 gram tracking force will thus have a potential skating force of .24 grams. We say *potential*, since, as noted above, if a tonearm's bearing friction is above .24 gram, it won't skate.

The bearing friction of the Dual 1009SK tonearm, on the other hand, is lower than 0.04 gram. Thus, Tracking-Balance Control of the same high order of precision—and with continuously variable control—was one of the major goals and achievements of the 1009SK's design.

Applying Tracking-Balance Control

Just as you set stylus force on the Dual with a continuously variable direct-reading dial, so do you set Tracking-Balance Control for that same force (Fig. 14).

Tracking Force	Tracking-Balance Control for Stylus Radii (in mils)					elliptical 0.2×0.9
	0.4	0.5	0.6	0.7	0.8	
0.5	0.70	0.60	0.50	0.50	0.45	0.85
1.0	1.25	1.15	1.00	0.95	0.90	1.50
1.5	1.80	1.60	1.50	1.45	1.40	2.10
2.0	2.30	2.10	2.00	1.95	1.90	2.70
2.5	2.90	2.60	2.50	2.45	2.40	3.40
3.0	3.50	3.10	3.00	2.90	2.85	4.20
3.5	4.10	3.65	3.50	3.40	3.35	
4.0	4.75	4.25	4.00	3.90	3.85	
4.5		4.75	4.50	4.35	4.30	
5.0		5.35	5.00	4.85	4.75	

As shown by the bold-face numerals in the chart, Tracking-Balance Control is calibrated for the most commonly used round stylus radius (0.6 mil). This calibration is also sufficiently accurate for other stylus radii as well.

What's more, for the perfectionist who wishes to take the fullest possible advantage of the precision Tracking-Balance Control now made possible, the other columns indicate the adjustment to be made for other radii from 0.4 mil to 0.8 mil, as well as the elliptical stylus (0.2 mil x 0.9 mil).

This means that for the first time you can *actually* balance stylus force on both walls of the stereo groove!

All this is one more example of how Dual assures you of the best possible performance from any cartridge/stylus combination.

INSTRUCTION

Instruction manuals are closely tied to extra-textual situations. They lead the reader through a series of processes, step by step. This kind of detail makes the instruction manual differ from more conventionally didactic texts, such as the Latin grammars, pages 125 through 128, which are designed to help the reader *remember* what he has been reading.

EXERCISES:

1. In "Operating Instructions", what are some of the most obvious grammatical, lexical and graphological markers of the functional tenor instruction?

2. What lexical items indicate a functional tenor, or tenors, other than instruction?

OPERATING INSTRUCTIONS

Needless to say, we are delighted that you have chosen the Dual 1009SK. Now, like most new owners, you are probably eager to get set up and play your first record. This won't take long, but it is important that you read the installation instructions carefully (on the inside of this flap). We also suggest you familiarize yourself with the 1009SK's many operating features as described on the following pages. Each of them is a typical example of Dual's advanced technology. Pleasant listening!

Master Operating Switch

This *one* feather-touch slide switch controls all operating functions, in both single play and changer operation, as described below. For automatic start, you move it past stop to start: For automatic stop, move it to stop. To start the platter rotating without putting the tonearm into cycle, move to manual after lifting tonearm from resting post and moving it toward the center.

Preparations for Play

Select the correct speed and record indexing size for the record to be played, then insert either the short spindle (for single play) or the Elevator-Action spindle (for changer operation).

Single Play

1. **Automatic Start:** move the slide switch to start.

2. **Automatic Start with Cue-Control.** First move Cue-Control to position ▼, then move slide switch to start. (This provides an even more gradual tonearm descent, as sometimes preferred for ultra high compliance cartridges.)

3. **Manual Start (on rotating record):**
   a. Lift tonearm and move switch to manual. (This can easily be done as shown in fig. 3.)
   b. Place tonearm on record.

4. **Manual Start (on motionless record):**
   a. Place tonearm on record.
   b. Move switch to manual.
   c. Move switch to manual.
   d. Flick Cue-Control to position ▼.

5. **Cue-Control Start (on rotating record):**
   a. Move Cue-Control to position ▼.
   b. Place tonearm over lead-in groove (or over any other groove).

6. **Cue-Control Start (on motionless record):**
   Same as 5, but reverse steps d and c.

7. **To stop play:** (tonearm returns to rest, motor shuts off)
   Push to stop.

8. **To interrupt play and replay from beginning:**
   Push gently to stop, pause, then continue to start.

9. **To interrupt play:** (when play is to be resumed where interrupted).
   Move Cue-Control to position ▼.

10. **To resume play:**
    Flick Cue-Control to position ▼.

NOTE: at the end of play, the tonearm will return to its resting post and the entire machine will shut off automatically.

Automatic Changer Operation

Insert the changer spindle by placing the key at its base into the slot of the shaft. Then turn the spindle clockwise *until it stops.* Up to ten records can be placed on the spindle.

All the functions for single play, as described above, are exactly the same in changer operation, plus these additional functions:

1. **To reject a record during play and change to the next record on the spindle:**
   Push gently to stop, pause, then continue to start.

2. **To skip the next record on the spindle:**
   Push to stop. After that record drops, push to start and the next record will drop.

NOTE: Any record already on the platter, can be replayed either automatically or manually, just as with the single play spindle. If there are any records on top of the one you wish to replay, simply lift them back onto the platform or off the spindle. (The 3-pronged platform will retract into the spindle as the records slip past.) No need to remove the spindle itself.

Jamproof Tonearm

During either single play or changer operation, the tonearm can be lifted from the record, moved and placed down again either by hand or by the Cue-Control. The tonearm may even be restrained during cycling without causing any malfunction . . . thanks to its foolproof slip-clutch.

INSTRUCTION AND ENCOURAGEMENT

Like the Dual instruction manual, the Canadian Government "Guide to the T1 Short" leads the reader through a process. But there is present in this text an equally important functional tenor: encouragement.

EXERCISES:

1. In this text, how are both of the functional tenors (instruction and encouragement) marked?

2. Compare the functional tenor of this text with that of the United States tax guide on the next page.

YOUR GUIDE
TO THE T1 SHORT
1970

a complete step-by-step guide to tax form filing . . . and many other tips for all *except* those:

(a) receiving rents, commissions or professional fees,

(b) with investment income over $2,500,

(c) in business as proprietors or partners, including farmers or fishermen,

(d) claiming foreign tax credits or capital cost allowance, or

(e) making additional Canada Pension Plan contributions as described in item 27 of this Guide.

(Individuals excepted above will use form T1 General.)

Follow this Guide . . . it will help you to avoid errors

Planning to claim medical expenses this year?

If you are planning to make a separate claim for medical expenses instead of claiming the standard deduction of $100, be sure to refer to item 14 of this Guide because, if you were covered by a provincial 'medicare' plan, certain expenses may not be claimed.

File only one personal income tax return

If, after filing your return, you realize that you made an error in your return or omitted some information that you should have included, do not file another return. Simply send a letter to your District Taxation Office (*not* to the Taxation Data Centre) advising of the error or omission. After your return is received from the Taxation Data Centre, the District Taxation Office will, if necessary, adjust your return and send you a Notice of Re-assessment.

How to use the income tax forms

First: Detach the T1 Short forms from the 4-page set.

Second: Complete the working copy of the form, following the instructions in this Guide as you go along. Be sure to enter every applicable detail and check your calculations.

Third: Copy the information from your working copy onto the copy that you are to mail, making sure that you complete both front and back of your mailing copy.

Fourth: Mail your signed return to the Taxation Data Centre, P.O. Box 456, Ottawa, using the pre-addressed envelope that is provided. If you owe tax, be sure to enclose your cheque or money order made out to the Receiver General for Canada. File your return by 30th April, 1971. The penalty for late filing is 5% of tax unpaid at 30th April, 1971.

Need more help?

A list of District Taxation Offices is provided in this Guide in case you need more information or wish to make an inquiry about your return. Inquiries by mail should be addressed to 'District Taxation Office', at the appropriate address, and *not* to the Taxation Data Centre.

Watch for announcements through local newspapers, radio and television about special information services available in your area during the filing period.

The material on this form is condensed from the Income Tax Act and Regulations and the Canada Pension Plan and Regulations which contain the terms of the law on which your tax and Canada Pension Plan contributions are determined.

You may find it helpful in preparing your Form 1040 for 1970 to follow these steps

1. Collect records relating to 1970 income including Forms W–2 and 1099.

2. Unless you are sure that you will not benefit by itemizing deductions, collect records of medical and dental expenses, charitable contributions, real estate taxes, State income tax, home mortgage interest, etc. See instruction, "Should You Use the Standard Deduction or Should You Itemize Your Deductions?" for line 19 on page 5.

3. Peel off mailing label and stick on the return you file. Check for and correct any errors in social security number, name and address.

4. Check filing status and enter exemptions (lines 1 through 11).

5. Follow lines 12 through 17. Complete any necessary supporting schedules for income and adjustments to arrive at adjusted gross income on line 18.

6. If you itemize deductions, fill out Schedule A.

7. If you do not itemize deductions and line 18 is under $10,000, find tax in Tax Tables 1 through 15. If you itemize deductions, or line 18 is $10,000 or more, fill in the tax computation, Part IV. In addition, use the Tax Surcharge Tables to figure your surcharge.

8. Check Parts V (Credits), VI (Other Taxes) and VII (Other Payments) on other side and carry totals to page 1. Enter withholding and estimated tax on page 1.

9. Compute balance due or overpayment.

10. Verify all entries, check arithmetic, and sign return.

You may have IRS compute your tax

If your income is under $10,000 and If your income on line 18 is $20,000 or less, and consists only of wages or salaries and tips, dividends, interest, pensions and annuities, and you choose the standard deduction instead of itemizing your actual deductions, you may have the Service figure your tax for you.

If you want the Service to do this, fill in lines 1 through 18, and 24, 26, 27, and 28. Skip lines 19 through 23, 25, and 29 through 32. If you are entitled to a retirement income credit, attach Schedule R, and enter "RIC" on line 22. If you are filing a joint return, show husband's and wife's income separately in the space to the left of the entry space for line 18. The Service will then compute your tax and refund any overpayment or bill you for any amount you owe.

Computing your tax in an uncomplicated situation

If your income is under $10,000 and consists only of wages and not more than $100 of dividends or interest (lines 12, 13c, and 14), and you are not itemizing your actual deductions, all the required entries for figuring your tax are on the front (page 1) of Form 1040. (You will need to make entries on page 2 and carry totals to the applicable lines on page 1 if your situation is more complicated and you claim adjustments on line 17, claim credits on line 22, owe other taxes on line 24, and claim payments against tax on lines 27 and 28.)

The following filled-in facsimile of Form 1040 gives an example showing you need make entries only on page 1 to figure your tax in a simple situation.

Example: John F. and Mary Brown have two (2) dependent children. Mr. Brown's Form W–2 shows wages of $9,875 and Federal income tax withheld of $1,096.42. They received $90 dividends from their joint stockholdings and $100 interest. Instead of itemizing their actual deductions they choose to find their tax in Tax Table 4, which has their standard deduction built in. Mr. and Mrs. Brown are filing a joint return and are claiming four (4) exemptions on line 11.

(Be sure to complete top of form (including lines 1 through 11) and the question at top of page 2)

SAMPLE FILLED-IN FORM

Income

12 Wages, salaries, tips, etc. (Attach Forms W–2 to back. If unavailable, attach explanation).	12	9,875	00 ★
13a Dividends (see pages 5 and 9 of instr.) $ 90.00 13b less exclusion $ 90.00 ...... Balance ▼	13c	0	
(Also list in Part II of Schedule B, if gross dividends and other distributions are over $100)			
14 Interest. Enter total here (also list in Part II of Schedule B, if total is over $100).	14	100	00 ★
15 Income other than wages, dividends, and interest (from line 40)	15	0	★
16 Total (add lines 12, 13c, 14 and 15).	16	9,975	00 ★
17 Adjustments to income (such as "sick pay," moving expense, etc., from line 45).	17	0	★
18 Adjusted gross income (subtract line 17 from line 16)	18	9,975	00 ★★

Tax and Surcharge

See page 2 of instructions for rules under which the IRS will figure your tax and surcharge.
If you do not itemize deductions and line 18 is under $10,000, find tax in Tables.
If you itemize deductions or line 18 is $10,000 or more, go to line 46 to figure tax.

19 Tax (Check if from: Tax Tables 1–15 ☒ Tax Rate Schedule X, Y, or Z ☐, Schedule D ☐, or Schedule G ☐). Enter tax on line 19.	19	1,091	00
20 Tax surcharge. See Tax Surcharge Tables A, B and C in instructions. (If you claim retirement income credit, use Schedule R to figure surcharge.)	20	27	00
21 Total (add lines 19 and 20).	21	1,118	00
22 Total credits (from line 55).	22	0	★
23 Income tax (subtract line 22 from line 21).	23	1,118	00
24 Other taxes (from line 61).	24	0	★
25 Total (add lines 23 and 24).	25	1,118	00 ★

Payments and Credits

26 Total Federal income tax withheld (attach Forms W–2 to back)	26	1,096	42
27 1970 Estimated tax payments (include 1969 overpayment allowed as a credit)	27		
28 Other payments (from line 65)	28		
29 Total (add lines 26, 27, and 28)	29	1,096	42

Due or Refund

30 If line 25 is larger than line 29, enter BALANCE DUE. Pay in full with return	30	21	58
31 If line 29 is larger than line 25, enter OVERPAYMENT	31		
32 Line 31 to be: (a) Credited on 1971 estimated tax ▶ $; (b) Refunded ▶ $			

DIDACTIC

Didactic writing attempts to teach the reader. In this selection from a Latin grammar such an intention is most clearly shown by logical organization and presentation. In section 21, for instance, a new technical term, "inflection", is introduced in bold upper-case type, clearly related to the field of discourse (Latin grammar), and immediately glossed.

EXERCISE:

The complexity of clause structure varies considerably in different parts of this text. Show how clause structure is related to the particular didactic task being attempted.

---

12   WORDS AND FORMS   [§§ 20-22

g. A **Conjunction** is a word which connects words, or groups of words, without affecting their grammatical relations: as, **et**, *and* ; **sed**, *but.*

NOTE. — Some adverbs are also used as connectives. These are called Adverbial Conjunctions or Conjunctive (Relative) Adverbs: as, **ubi**, *where*; **dōnec**, *until.*

h. **Interjections** are mere exclamations and are not strictly to be classed as parts of speech. Thus, — **heus**, *halloo!* **ō**, *oh!*

NOTE. — Interjections sometimes express an emotion which affects a person or thing mentioned, and so have a grammatical connection like other words: as, **vae victīs**, *woe to the conquered* (alas for the conquered)!

INFLECTION

21. Latin is an *inflected language.*

Inflection is a change made in the form of a word to show its grammatical relations.

a. Inflectional changes sometimes take place in the body of a word, or at the beginning, but oftener in its termination: —

vōx, *a voice*; **vōcis**, *of a voice*; **vocō**, *I call*; **vocat**, *he calls*; **vocet**, *let him call*; **vocāvit**, *he has called*; **tangit**, *he touches*; **tetigit**, *he touched.*

b. **Terminations** of inflection had originally independent meanings which are now obscured. They correspond nearly to the use of prepositions, auxiliaries, and personal pronouns in English.

Thus, in **vocat**, the termination is equivalent to *he* or *she*; in **vōcis**, to the preposition *of*; and in **vocet** the change of vowel signifies a change of mood.

c. Inflectional changes in the body of a verb usually denote relations of tense or mood, and often correspond to the use of auxiliary verbs in English: —

frangit, *he breaks* or *is breaking* ; **frēgit**, *he broke* or *has broken* ; **mordet**, *he bites* ; **momordit**, *he bit.*[1]

22. The inflection of Nouns, Adjectives, Pronouns, and Participles to denote gender, number, and case is called **Declension**, and these parts of speech are said to be *declined.*

The inflection of Verbs to denote voice, mood, tense, number, and person is called **Conjugation**, and the verb is said to be *conjugated.*

NOTE. — Adjectives are often said to have inflections of *comparison.* These are, however, properly stem-formations made by derivation (p. 55, footnote).

[1] The only *proper* inflections of verbs are those of the personal endings; and the changes here referred to are strictly changes of *stem*, but have become a part of the system of inflections.

23. Adverbs, Prepositions, Conjunctions, and Interjections are not inflected and are called Particles.

NOTE. — The term Particle is sometimes limited to such words as num, -ne, an (*interrogative*), nōn, nē (*negative*), sī (*conditional*), etc., which are used simply to indicate the form or construction of a sentence.

Root, Stem, and Base

24. The body of a word, to which the terminations are attached, is called the Stem.

The Stem contains the *idea* of the word without relations ; but, except in the first part of a compound (as, **arti-fex**, *artificer*), it cannot ordinarily be used without some termination to express them.[1]

Thus the stem **vōc-** denotes *voice* ; with **-s** added it becomes **vōx**, *a voice* or *the voice*, as the subject or agent of an action ; with **-is** it becomes **vōcis**, *and signifies of a voice*.

NOTE. — The stem is in many forms so united with the termination that a comparison with other forms is necessary to determine it.

25. A Root is the simplest form attainable by analysis of a word into its component parts.

Such a form contains the main idea of the word in a very general sense, and is common also to other words either in the same language or in kindred languages.[2]

Thus the root of the stem **vōc-** is voc, which does not mean *to call*, or *I call*, or *calling*, but merely expresses vaguely the idea of calling, and cannot be used as a part of speech without terminations. With **ā-** it becomes **vocā-**, the stem of **vocāre** (*to call*) ; with **āv-** it is the stem of **vocāvit** (*he called*) ; with **āto-** it becomes the stem of **vocātus** (*called*) ; with **ātiōn-** it becomes the stem of **vocātiōnis** (*of a calling*). With its vowel lengthened it becomes the stem of **vōx**, **vōc-is** (*a voice* : that by which we call). This stem **vōc-**, with **-ālis** added, means *belonging to a voice* ; with **-ŭla**, *a little voice*.

NOTE. — In inflected languages, words are built up from Roots, which at a very early time were used alone to express ideas, as is now done in Chinese. Roots are modified into Stems, which, by inflection, become fully formed words. The process by which roots are modified, in the various forms of derivatives and compounds, is called *Stem-building*. The whole of this process is originally one of composition, by which significant endings are added one after another to forms capable of pronunciation and conveying a meaning.

Roots had long ceased to be recognized as such before the Latin existed as a separate language. Consequently the forms which we assume as Latin roots never really existed in Latin, but are the representatives of forms used earlier.

---

[1] Another exception is the imperative second person singular in **-e** (as, **rege**).

[2] For example, the root SrA is found in the Sanskrit *tishthāmi*, Greek ἵστημι, Latin **sistere** and **stāre**, German ſtehen, and English *stand*.

DIDACTIC

In the excerpt from Latin grammar below, the functional tenor didactic is marked at the lexical level. Two lexical sets establish the fields of discourse: "Roman empire" and "Latin language and literature". "Power", although not itself the field of discourse at any point, provides an essential connection between "Roman empire" and "Latin language and literature" which influences the reader's attitude towards Latin literature.

POWER

LATIN GRAMMAR

INTRODUCTION

§ 1 THE Romans were one of the great imperial races of the Ancient World, and Latin was their language. Originally Rome was no more than an outpost of the Latin tribes, and Latin no more than a rude dialect. After many years of struggle Rome became mistress first of Italy and, by the time of Julius Caesar (last century B.C.) mistress of the countries that lie round the Mediterranean. As the Romans grew richer more powerful and more ambitious and came into contact with older peoples like the Greeks, who had a literature of their own, they sought to give Latin a literary form and to make a national Roman literature. They succeeded. Latin literature reached its highest point in the century before and the century after the beginning of our era. Their greatest writers of that period have had an immense influence on the literature of the modern world. Cicero in oratory; Lucretius, Virgil, Horace, and Ovid in poetry; Caesar, Livy and Tacitus in history, have not only told us much about what the Romans did, thought, hoped, or dreamed of, but have set up models of literary achievement.

§ 2 But the importance of Latin does not end there. The influence of Rome was particularly strong in what is now Italy, France, Spain, and England, and Latin became, and for hundreds of years continued to be, the only common language understood throughout these lands. When Christianity came, Latin both helped it to spread and was

EXERCISE:

Assume that you are a teacher in nation X in the year 2950, and that you want to have students study Canadian language and literature. Write an "Introduction" to *Canadian Grammar*. Before doing so, read through this text substituting "Canadian" and "Canada" for "Latin" and "Rome". Instead of the value "power", you might wish to focus on "thrift", "industry", "sturdy independence", "peacefulness" or some other inspiring attribute.

DIDACTIC

"What is Latin?" overtly announces its didacticism. In its first paragraph, the field of discourse is the *learning* process.

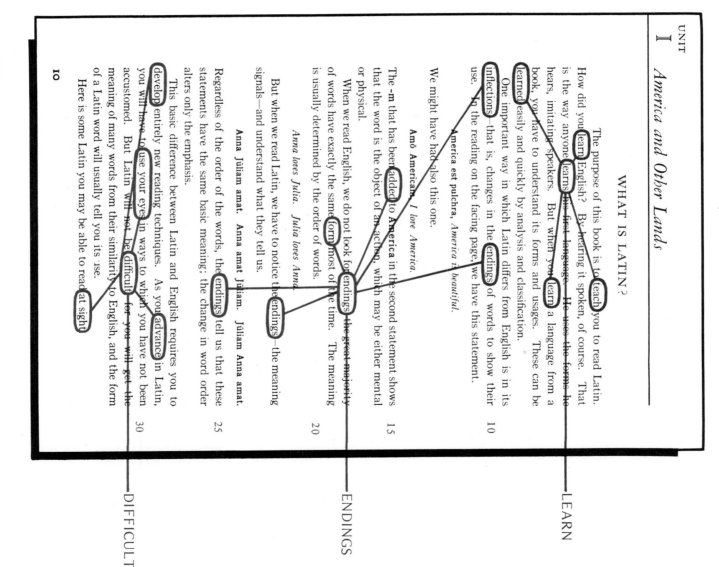

UNIT

I *America and Other Lands*

WHAT IS LATIN?

How did you learn English? By hearing it spoken, of course. That is the way anyone learns the first language. He uses the forms he hears, imitating speakers. But when you learn a language from a book, you have to understand its forms and usages. These can be learned easily and quickly by analysis and classification.

One important way in which Latin differs from English is in its inflections—that is, changes in the endings of words to show their use. In the reading on the facing page, we have this statement.

America est pulchra, America is beautiful.

We might have had also this one.

Amō Americam, I love America.

The **-m** that has been added to **America** in the second statement shows that the word is the object of an action, which may be either mental or physical.

When we read English, we do not look for endings the great majority of words have exactly the same form most of the time. The meaning is usually determined by the order of words.

Anna loves Julia. Julia loves Anna.

But when we read Latin, we have to notice the endings—the meaning signals—and understand what they tell us.

Anna Jūliam amat. Anna amat Jūliam. Jūliam Anna amat.

Anna loves Julia.

Regardless of the order of the words, the endings tell us that these statements have the same basic meaning; the change in word order alters only the emphasis.

This basic difference between Latin and English requires you to develop entirely new reading techniques. As you advance in Latin, you will have to use your eyes in ways to which you have not been accustomed. But Latin will not be difficult for you if you get the meaning of many words from their similarity to English, and the form of a Latin word will usually tell you its use.

Here is some Latin you may be able to read at sight.

10

5

15

20

25

30

LEARN

ENDINGS

DIFFICULT

EXERCISE:

Contrast this text with the two previous ones in terms of field, mode, personal tenor, graphology, lexis, and grammar. Be specific in listing markers.

DIATYPIC ANALYSIS

So far in Part Two, the diatypic varieties have been illustrated one at a time. You have examined each text in terms of a single, clearly marked dimension (field, mode, personal tenor, or functional tenor).

The following eight texts are marked in a complex way. Some have interesting combinations of functional tenors, while others are highly marked for more than one dimension.

"Information Builds Profit" (page 130) achieves three important functions of an advertisement: it informs, it persuades, and, as a prelude to these, it arrests the attention of the reader. The reader's attention is attracted by all three parts of the advertisement. The carefully balanced opening sentences, "Information builds profit" and "Olivetti builds information", in which parallelism achieved in grammar, lexis, and use of graphic resources, not only secure the reader's interest, but also lead him inescapably to the conclusion that "Olivetti builds profit".

Interest is sustained by the staccato effect of the series of minor clause sentences, while at the same time, a great deal of factual information is presented. The heads of the groups ("calculators", "typewriters", "machines", "computers", "terminals", "teleprinters", "systems", and "photocopiers") form a lexical set. Even skimming over them, the reader is aware of a wide range of office equipment. Balanced pairs of modifiers ("electric" and "manual", "desk-top" and "office", "magnetic" and "optional character") reinforce the impression of wide range; while the involved, heavily rankshifted "magnetic and optical character document handling", all of which modifies "systems", is persuasive because it *convinces*, in that it is characteristic of scientific prose.

The block at the bottom is the most interesting part of the advertisement. The dominant feature is the distinctive O of the Olivetti trademark, which has been cut up, turned around, and generally distributed to awaken interest, much like the use of graphic resources in concrete poetry. The collage is made up largely of the actual keys of various machines, and the symbols on them are mainly numbers. The inclusion of the symbol for the British pound is persuasive, not only because it relates to "profits" in the first line, but also because it suggests the international clientele of Olivetti.

INFORMATION BUILDS PROFIT
OLIVETTI BUILDS INFORMATION

Electric and electronic printing calculators
Electric and manual typewriters
Accounting and invoicing machines
Desk-top and office computers
Terminals and teleprinters
Data assembly and controlled transmission systems
Magnetic and optical character document handling systems
Electrostatic photocopiers

olivetti

Shifts of functional tenor are not usually as sharply defined as in this text, taken from the 11th edition *Encyclopaedia Britannica*.

NEBORG—ABORTION   67

rsity has
e ecclesias-
rchbishop
d restored
St Henry,
who intro-
tury. Åbo
f Finland.
school of
r its trade;
there are
mber and
nsiderably
sian navy.
t ships of
our (Born-
by from

. corner of
al area of
f 447,098,
, 446,900
a promi-
ons, sugar
&c. Its
), Raumo
917).

t for," to
has a more
icate the
be either
r certain
on busi-
term has
has been
sleeps, at

or ceremonial practices which were impure. An incorrect derivation was *ab homine* (*i.e.* inhuman), and the spelling of the adjective "abominable" in the first Shakespeare folio is always "abominable." Colloquially "abomination" and "abominable" are used to mean simply excessive in a disagreeable sense.

ABOR HILLS, a tract of country on the north-east frontier of India, occupied by an independent tribe called the Abors. It lies north of Lakhimpur district, in the province of eastern Bengal and Assam, and is bounded on the east by the Mishmi Hills and on the west by the Miri Hills, the villages of the tribe extending to the Dibong river. The term Abor is an Assamese word, signifying "barbarous" or "independent," and is applied in a general sense by the Assamese to many frontier tribes; but in its restricted sense it is specially given to the above tract. The Abors, together with the cognate tribes of Miris, Daphlas and Akas, are supposed to be descended from a Tibetan stock. They are a quarrelsome and sulky race, violently divided in their political relations. In former times they committed frequent raids upon the plains of Assam, and have been the object of more than one retaliatory expedition by the British government. In 1893–94 occurred the first Bor Abor expedition. Some military police sepoys were murdered in British territory, and a force of 600 troops was sent, who traversed the Abor country, and destroyed the villages concerned in the murder and all other villages that opposed the expedition. A second expedition became necessary later on, two small patrols having been treacherously murdered; and a force of 100 British troops traversed the border of the Abor country and punished the tribes, while a blockade was continued against them from 1894 to 1900.
See Colonel Dalton's *Ethnology of Bengal*, 1872.

ABORIGINES, a mythical people of central Italy, connected in legendary history with Aeneas, Latinus and Evander. They were supposed to have descended from their mountain home near Reate (an ancient Sabine town) upon Latium, whence they expelled the Siceli and subsequently settled down as Latini under a King Latinus (Dion. Halic. i. 9. 60). The most gener-

5

10

15

20

25

EXERCISES:

1. Find lexical evidence for the shift from expository to another functional tenor.

2. The encyclopaedia-reader relationship constitutes a "situation" relevant to the analysis of "Abor Hills". Discuss the appropriateness of each of the two functional tenors in this text to the situation.

3. Briefly describe a situation in which the functional tenor of the second portion of the text is appropriate. (This does not imply that you agree or disagree with the writer's point of view.)

This text could be seen as a narrative account of the development of Freud's thought, but the functional tenors of exposition and evaluation are also present.

EVALUATION OF FREUD'S BIOLOGICAL ORIENTATION   45

energy did not go out from a person and become attached to another, it seemed logical to suppose it remained attached to the person's own ego.

Freud assumed that originally a quantum of sexual energy was attached to every organ in the body. Such, he said, is the condition of the organism at birth. This is primary narcissism. However, he thought there was no way of measuring this energy except as we presumably can observe it going out and becoming attached to another organism. In doing this the narcissistic libido becomes converted into object libido and a bond is formed between the two people. This is object love.   10

It is important to keep in mind that Freud thought of this libido as a quantity. If a part of one's libido becomes attached to another person, then the individual has lost it. Freud says that is why a man in love suffers from feelings of   15
unworthiness.[1] He has lost some of his self-love. His ego is poorer in libido. If his love is successful, he gets a quantity of libido back from the other and self-esteem is restored. If a person is rebuffed or falls out of love, his libido then returns to himself and becomes once more attached to his own body.   20
This is secondary narcissism—the return of one's libido to oneself after rebuff. One is again rich in self-love. Primary narcissism Freud saw as healthy; secondary narcissism is always the result of failure to make an object attachment. This   25
is a perfectly consistent theory given the premise that life is dominated by the distribution of libido. However, it puts one in the untenable position of saying that the narcissist is a richer person than the individual capable of love.   30

[1] *Collected Papers*, Vol. IV, Ch. 3.

EXERCISES:

1.   Show markers of the narrative framework.

2.   Show markers of the field of discourse Freudian psychology.

3.   Show markers of the author's evaluation of Freudian psychology.

The basic functional tenor of this "Preface" is narrative — it has the title "History", and it consistently uses the past tense.

PREFACE

HISTORY

❧ The *Guide to Reference Books* has had a long and notable history. Begun in 1902, when the American Library Association published the *Guide to the Study and.*
5 *Use of Reference Books* by Alice Bertha Kroeger, this pioneer work achieved an immediate success and was soon adopted as a textbook in library schools and training classes. Annual supplements for 1903 to 1907 were printed in the *Library Journal*, and in the fall of 1908,
10 a second edition, revised and considerably enlarged, was issued. Miss Kroeger, who for many years had taught reference work in the Drexel Institute Library School in Philadelphia, died in 1909.
In 1910 the Publishing Board of the American Library
15 Association asked Isadore Gilbert Mudge to continue the *Guide*. Thus began a connection which lasted for almost

thirty years, and included the third to the sixth editions, of 1917, 1923, 1929, and 1936, with intervening supplements. Miss Mudge became the outstanding authority
20 on reference books, and her *Guide* was known and consulted in libraries throughout the world. She was particularly well fitted for the work by her long experience both as a teacher and as a reference librarian: at the University of Illinois, at Bryn Mawr College, at Simmons Col-
25 lege, and finally at Columbia University, where she was Reference Librarian from 1911 to 1941 and Associate Professor in the School of Library Service from 1926 to 1938. Her thorough familiarity with reference books and reference techniques, her clear thinking, her wide
30 knowledge and remarkable memory, her deep interest in the subject and in the student and research worker, all combined to impress her influence on succeeding generations of students, faculty, and all those who used her

v

EXERCISE:

Show that this "Preface" has praise as a highly marked second functional tenor.

EVERGREEN REVIEW

315 HUDSON STREET, NEW YORK, N. Y. 10013

EDITORIAL OFFICES

"alive and burning..."

Five Remarkable Books FREE on this Anniversary (including Ok! Calcutta!)

Dear Reader:

✓ A University Professor tells about his astonishing interviews on MARIJUANA & SEX with 200 users . . .

5

✓ Eldridge Cleaver raps in a no-holds-barred interview with Evergreen . . .

✓ Timothy Leary takes you on a guided visit to turned-on Anglo-India, a hip session of London's Parliament and the Beatles' revelations . . .

10

✓ The Director of the sensational Swedish film, I am Curious (yellow), reveals the diary he kept during the making of this film . . .

15

✓ A Frenchman Looks at Erotica -- The "outrageously brilliant little monster of a play", The Beard -- Behind the moviemaking scenes with Warhol -- A Portfolio of full-color photographs of EP (epidermal) Art in the making . . .

20

Exciting? Yes! Provocative? Yes! Fresh and literate? Yes! That's the cultural explosion every month in the pages of Evergreen Review, where the world's most gifted writers, artists, playwrights and photographers deliver themselves "... alive and burning onto the printed page", to quote Newsweek.

Now Evergreen's Editors have arranged
to send you five remarkable books
FREE on this Anniversary occasion.

25

This richly rewarding gift is our way of inviting you to celebrate Evergreen Review's Anniversary with us -- to enjoy each month a fresh, eye-opening experience, with more good reading, more stunning photos, more dazzling visual delights than you've ever seen before.

30

And this gift represents the feeling of our Editors that YOU, unless we have been badly misinformed, would share with over 200,000 readers a delight in the most adult - the most literate - the most stimulating and meaningful writing, theatre, art and photography on today's cultural scene.

35

- 2 -

Under this very special invitation, you receive --

✓ An introductory subscription to the monthly Evergreen Review at a saving of 25¢ from the newsstand price (or 33% off if you prefer the longer term);

✓ PLUS copies of any three of the outstanding books shown on the enclosed announcement - sent to you at once with the Editors' compliments. The choice is yours. 40

(For example, you may choose the richly exciting new 500-page ROMANCE OF LUST . . .the newly published autobiographical volume, SUBURBAN SOULS, one of the three most rare sexual memoirs ever printed . .six volumes complete in one mammoth book) . . the smash hit Oh! Calcutta! with 60 on-stage photographs . . . or any of the other four volumes shown to make up your three-book Bonus.) 45 / 50

✓ PLUS the additional gift of VENUS SCHOOL-MISTRESS to mark this Anniversary occasion;

(AND AN EXTRA BONUS)

✓ The fifth book is I AM CURIOUS, which makes available the scenario and over 250 still photos from the sensational Swedish film. It is yours as an extra free bonus simply for saving us and you the bother of bookkeeping and billing on your introductory subscription. 55

This is a perfect opportunity to start enjoying the new cultural explosion in the pages of Evergreen Review. You not only receive the most tuned-in and consistently stimulating magazine on the scene today, (at a substantial saving), but you also get the unprecedented Anniversary bonus of five out-standing books free. 60

All you need do is return the enclosed subscription voucher today in the postpaid envelope. Your free bonus books will go out to you at once. 65

Sincerely,

Myron Shapiro
For the Board of Editors

P.S. And here's a wonderful "extra" . . . As a subscriber to Evergreen Review, you will also receive full benefits of membership in Evergreen Club, the only club of its kind which makes available honest, powerful, and adult books which may never show up in your corner bookstore. Members never have to buy any book ever, but if they do, they benefit from unusually low Club prices. Your membership is completely free. 70 / 75

EXERCISES:

1. This is obviously a written text. What graphic elements defy translation to the spoken mode? What graphological features contribute to the functional tenor?

2. How is the functional tenor marked by grammar and lexis?

3. Find markers for the informal personal tenor, which contributes to the persuasive effect.

EXERCISE:

At first glance, "Split Infinitive", an entry from Fowler's *A Dictionary of Modern English Usage*, seems to be expository. It occurs, however, in a book designed to teach the reader how to speak and write "properly". Discuss the features which mark the text as expository. Discuss markers of other functional tenors, such as blame, praise, and amusement. What relation do these tenors bear to instruction?

---

male or female attire & discard its other garments; on this point cf. NAIF & NAIVE. On the other hand, [5] the choice is with this particular word a dilemma; if we decide for -*el* we are sacrificing the much more familiar of the two forms—more familiar because the word has been [10] chiefly applied to women & in this application purposely made feminine by those who recognize both genders; but, if we decide for -*elle*, few of us can rid themselves of the [15] feeling that the word is feminine & suitable only to what, for the English, is alone feminine, viz woman, so that we find ourselves debarred from describing qualities, faces, talk, [20] & above all men, as spirituelle, & cannot give the word its proper extension.

The lesser evil is to spell always *spirituel*; the objection to it is not, [25] like that to -*elle*, one that will endure for ever, but one that, when the form is settled, will no longer be felt.

spirt, spurt. The spelling is now [30] very much a matter of personal fancy, & whether more than one word is concerned is doubtful. There are, however, two distinguishable main senses—that of gush, jet, or [35] flow (vb & n.), & that of sprint, burst, hustle (vb & n.); & for the second sense the form *spurt* is far the commoner. It would plainly be convenient if the DIFFERENTIATION [40] thus indicated were made absolute; *a spirt of blood; works by spurts; oil spirts up; Jones spurted past.*

spite makes *spiteful*; see MUTE E.
splay. For inflexions see VERBS IN [45] -IE &c., 1.
splendid makes -*idest*; -ER & -EST 4.
splendiferous. See FACETIOUS FORMATIONS.
splendo(u)r. Keep the u; but see [50] -OUR & -OR.
splice makes -*ceable*; see -ABLE 1.
SPLIT INFINITIVE. The English-speaking world may be divided into (1) those who neither know nor care [55] what a split infinitive is; (2) those

who do not know, but care very much; (3) those who know & condemn; (4) those who know & approve; & (5) those who know & [60] distinguish.

1. Those who neither know nor care are the vast majority, & are a happy folk, to be envied by most of the minority classes; 'to really [65] understand' comes readier to their lips & pens than 'really to understand', they see no reason why they should not say it (small blame to them, seeing that reasons are not [70] their critics' strong point), & they do say it, to the discomfort of some among us, but not to their own.

2. To the second class, those who do not know but do care, who would [75] as soon be caught putting their knives in their mouths as splitting an infinitive but have hazy notions of what constitutes that deplorable breach of etiquette, this article is [80] chiefly addressed. These people betray by their practice that their aversion to the split infinitive springs not from instinctive good taste, but from tame acceptance of [85] the misinterpreted opinion of others; for they will subject their sentences to the queerest distortions, all to escape imaginary split infinitives. 'To really understand' is as.i.; 'to [90] really be understood' is a s.i.; 'to be really understood' is not one; to grasp that distinction is incredible. Those upon whom the fear of infinitive-splitting sits heavy should [95] remember that to give conclusive evidence, by distortions, of misconceiving the nature of the s.i. is far more damaging to their literary pretensions than an actual lapse could [100] be; for it exhibits them as deaf to the normal rhythm of English sentences. No sensitive ear can fail to be shocked, if the following examples are read aloud, by the [105] strangeness of the indicated adverbs. Why on earth, the reader wonders, is that word out of its place? He will find, on looking through again, [110]

that each has been turned out of a similar position, viz between the word *be* & a passive participle. Reflection will assure him that the cause of dislocation is always the same—all these writers have sacrificed the run of their sentences to the delusion that 'to be really understood' is a split infinitive. It is not; & the straitest non-splitter of us all can with a clear conscience restore each of the adverbs to its rightful place:—He was proposed at the last moment as a candidate likely *generally* to be accepted./ When the record of this campaign comes *dispassionately* to be written, & in just perspective, it will be found that . . ./The leaders have given instructions that the lives & property of foreigners shall *scrupulously* be respected./New principles will have *boldly* to be adopted if the Scottish case is to be met./This is a very serious matter, which clearly ought *further* to be inquired into./ There are many points raised in the report which need *carefully* to be explored./Only two ways of escaping from the conflict without loss, by this time become too serious *squarely* to be faced, have ever offered themselves./The Headmaster of a public school possesses very great powers, which ought *most carefully* & *considerately* to be exercised./The time to get this revaluation put through is when the amount paid by the State to the localities is *very largely* to be increased./But the party whose Leader in the House of Commons acts in this way cannot fail *deeply* to be discredited by the way in which he flings out & about these false charges.

3. The above writers are bogy-haunted creatures who for fear of splitting an infinitive abstain from doing something quite different, i.e. dividing *be* from its complement by an adverb; see further under POSITION OF ADVERBS. Those who presumably do know what split infinitives are, & condemn them, are not so easily identified, since they in-

clude all who neither commit the sin nor flounder about in saving themselves from it, all who combine with acceptance of conventional rules a reasonable dexterity. But when the dexterity is lacking, disaster follows. It does not add to a writer's readableness if readers are pulled up now & again to wonder— Why this distortion? Ah, to be sure, a non-split die-hard! That is the mental dialogue occasioned by each of the adverbs in the examples below. It is of no avail merely to fling oneself desperately out of temptation; one must so do it that no traces of the struggle remain; that is, sentences must be thoroughly remodelled instead of having a word lifted from its original place & dumped elsewhere:—What alternative can be found which the Pope has not condemned, & which will make it possible *to organize legally* public worship?/If it is to do justice between the various parties & not *unduly to burden* the State, it will . . ./It will, when better understood, tend *firmly to establish* relations between Capital & Labour./Both Germany & England have done ill in not combining *to forbid flatly* hostilities./Nobody expects that the executive of the Amalgamated Society is going *to assume publicly* sackcloth & ashes./Every effort must be made *to increase adequately* professional knowledge & attainments./We have had *to shorten somewhat* Lord Denbigh's letter./The kind of sincerity which enables an author *to move powerfully* the heart would . . ./Safeguards should be provided *to prevent effectually* cosmopolitan financiers from manipulating these reserves.

4. Just as those who know & condemn the s.i. include many who are not recognizable, only the clumsier performers giving positive proof of resistance to temptation, so too those who know & approve are not distinguishable with certainty; when a man splits an infinitive, he may be doing it unconsciously as a member of our class 1, or he may be

138

deliberately rejecting the trammels
of convention & announcing that he
means to do as he will with his own
infinitives. But, as the following
examples are from newspapers of 230
high repute, & high newspaper tradition is strong against splitting, it
is perhaps fair to assume that each
specimen is a manifesto of independence :—It will be found possible 235
to considerably improve the present
wages of the miners without jeopar-
dizing the interests of capital./
Always providing that the Im-
perialists do not feel strong enough 240
to decisively assert their power in
the revolted provinces./But even so,
he seems *to still be allowed* to speak
at Unionist demonstrations./It is
the intention of the Minister of 245
Transport *to substantially increase*
all present rates by means of a
general percentage./The men in
many of the largest districts are
declared *to strongly favour* a strike if 250
the minimum wage is not conceded.
It should be noticed that in these
the separating adverb could have
been placed outside the infinitive
with little or in most cases no 255
damage to the sentence-rhythm
(*considerably* after *miners, decisively*
after *powers, still* with clear gain
after *be, substantially* after *rates,* &
strongly at some loss after *strike*), so 260
that protest seems a safe diagnosis.
5. The attitude of those who know
& distinguish is something like this :
We admit that separation of *to* from
its infinitive (viz *be, do, have, sit,* 265
doubt, kill, or other verb) inflexionally
similar) is not in itself desirable,
& we shall not gratuitously say
either 'to mortally wound' or 'to
mortally be wounded' ; but we are 270
not foolish enough to confuse the
latter with 'to be mortally wounded,'
which is blameless English, nor 'to
just have heard' with 'to have just
heard', which is also blameless. 275
We maintain, however, that a real
s. i., though not desirable in itself,
is preferable to either of two things,
to real ambiguity, & to patent
artificiality. For the first, we will

rather write 'Our object is to
further cement trade relations'
than, by correcting into 'Our object
is further to cement . . .', leave it
doubtful whether an additional 285
object or additional cementing is the
point. And for the second, we take
it that such reminders of a tyrannous
convention as 'in not combining
to forbid flatly hostilities' are far 290
more abnormal than the abnor-
mality they evade. We will split
infinitives sooner than be ambiguous
or artificial ; more than that, we
will freely admit that sufficient 295
recasting will get rid of any s. i.
without involving either of those
faults, & yet reserve to ourselves
the right of deciding in each case
whether recasting is worth while. 300
Let us take an example : 'In these
circumstances, the Commission,
judging from the evidence taken in
London, has been feeling its way
to modifications intended to better 305
equip successful candidates for
careers in India & at the same time
to meet reasonable Indian demands'.
To better equip ? We refuse 'better
to equip' as a shouted reminder of 310
the tyranny ; we refuse 'to equip
better' as ambiguous (*better* an
adjective ?) ; we regard 'to equip
successful candidates better' as
lacking compactness, as possibly 315
tolerable from an anti-splitter, but
not good enough for us. What then
of recasting ? 'intended to make
successful candidates fitter for' is
the best we can do i' the exact sense 320
is to be kept ; it takes some thought
to arrive at the correction ; was the
game worth the candle ?
After this inconclusive discussion,
in which, however, the author's 325
opinion has perhaps been allowed
to appear with indecent plainness,
readers may like to settle for themselves whether, in the following sentence, 'either to secure' followed 330
by 'to resign', or 'to either secure'
followed by 'resign', should have
been preferred—an issue in which
the meaning & the convention are
pitted against each other :—The 335

speech has drawn an interesting letter from Sir Antony MacDonnell, who states that his agreement with Mr Wyndham was never cancelled, & that Mr Long was too weak *either to secure* the dismissal of Sir Antony or himself to resign office.

It is perhaps hardly fair that this article should have quoted no split infinitives except such as, being reasonably supposed (as in 4) to be deliberate, are likely to be favourable specimens. Let it therefore conclude with one borrowed from a reviewer, to whose description of it no exception need be taken : ' A book . . . of which the purpose is thus—with a deafening split infinitive—stated by its author :—" Its main idea is *to* historically, even while events are maturing, & divinely—from the Divine point of view—*impeach* the European system of Church & States ".'.

SPLIT VERBS. *There can be little doubt that the position of his troops all the way from Berat northward will seriously be imperilled.* For questions such as that suggested by the last four words of this, see POSITION OF ADVERBS, 4.

splodge, splotch. The second is two centuries older ; the first perhaps now more usual & felt to be more descriptive ; cf. SLUSH, & SMUDGE.

splutter, sputter. Without any clear or constant difference of meaning, it may be said that in *sputter* the notion of spitting is more insistent, & that it tends on that account to be avoided when that notion is not essential.

spoil. For *spoiled, -lt*, see -T & -ED. **-spoken.** For the curious use in *fair, free, soft, out, &c., -s* (where *soft-speeched* &c. might have been expected), see INTRANSITIVE P.P. It should be remembered that in these compounds *fair-* &c. are adverbial as much as *out-*, & that what is remarkable is not the adverbial use of the adjective, but the active use of the participle.

spondee. See TECHNICAL TERMS.
sponge makes *spongeable*, see -ABLE 1 ; but *sponging* & *spongy*, see MUTE E.
spontaneity, -ousness. -TY & -NESS.
spook. Pronounce -ook.
spoondrift. See SPINDRIFT.
spoon(e)y. The adjective should be -*ny*, see -EY & -Y ; for the noun, in which either is legitimate, & -*ey* probably more frequent, -EY, -IE, -Y.
spoonful. Pl. *spoonfuls* ; see -FUL.
spouse. For the use in ordinary writing in preference to *wife*, see FORMAL WORDS ; but s. is serviceable as short for husband-or-wife in some styles, e.g. in dictionaries or legal documents.
sprain)(strain. It is natural to wish for a clear line of distinction between two words that, as applied to bodily injuries, are so near in sense & both so well established ; but even in medical books they are often treated as equivalent. *Sprain*, perhaps, describes the result rather of a momentary wrench or twist, & *strain* that of an exertion of muscle too strong or too long for its capacity.
spray, nn., make *sprayey* ; see -EY & -Y, exception 1.
spray, vb. For inflexions see VERBS IN -IE &c., 1.
spring. The past *sprang* is considerably more frequent than *sprung*, both in trans. & in intrans. senses.
spring, n. The compounds, like those of SEA, are of interest to the hyphen-fancier. For the principle, see HYPHENS 3 B ; *spring-bed, spring-mattress, spring-gun*, are usually forbidden by the accent, & must be changed to two words each; *spring-time* & *spring-board* are allowed by accent, unless *springtime* & *springboard* are preferred ; *springtide* or *springtide* can stand only for the season, & the tidal term must be *spring tide* in two words ; *spring(-) cart* will usually be two words, but may be hyphened when all the stress is on *spring* & a spring-cart is to be distinguished from other carts & not from vehicles in general.

This excerpt from Harold Pinter's *The Lover* is an accurate imitation of the patterns of spoken speech. Yet the reader recognizes it as absurd. Why? The answer is apparent when the text is analyzed in terms of the diatypic varieties.

THE LOVER was first presented by Associated-Rediffusion Television, London, March 28th, 1963, with the following cast:

RICHARD	Alan Badel
SARAH	Vivien Merchant
JOHN	Michael Forrest

Directed by Joan Kemp-Welch

The play was first presented on the stage by Michael Codron and David Hall at the Arts Theatre, September 18th, 1963, with the following cast:

RICHARD	Scott Forbes
SARAH	Vivien Merchant
JOHN	Michael Forrest

Directed by Harold Pinter

Assisted by Guy Vaesen

Summer. A detached house near Windsor

The stage consists of two areas. Living-room right, with small hall and front door up centre. Bedroom and balcony, on a level, left. There is a short flight of stairs to bedroom door. Kitchen off right. A table with a long velvet cover stands against the left wall of the living-room, centre stage. In the small hall there is a cupboard. The furnishings are tasteful, comfortable.

SARAH is emptying and dusting ashtrays in the living-room. It is morning. She wears a crisp, demure dress. RICHARD comes into the bedroom from bathroom, off left, collects his briefcase from hall cupboard, goes to SARAH, kisses her on the cheek. He looks at her for a moment smiling. She smiles.

RICHARD (*amiably*). Is your lover coming today?
SARAH. Mmnn.
RICHARD. What time?
SARAH. Three.
RICHARD. Will you be going out . . . or staying in?
SARAH. Oh . . . I think we'll stay in.
RICHARD. I thought you wanted to go to that exhibition.
SARAH. I did, yes . . . but I think I'd prefer to stay in with him today.
RICHARD. Mmn-hmmn. Well, I must be off.

He goes to the hall and puts on his bowler hat.

RICHARD. Will he be staying long do you think?
SARAH. Mmmnnn . . .
RICHARD. About . . . six, then.
SARAH. Yes.
RICHARD. Have a pleasant afternoon.
SARAH. Mmnn.
RICHARD. Bye-bye.
SARAH. Bye.

C–D

THE LOVER

He opens the front door and goes out. She continues dusting. The lights fade.
Fade up. Early evening. SARAH comes into room from kitchen. She wears the same dress, but is now wearing a pair of very high-heeled shoes. She pours a drink and sits on chaise longue with magazine. There are six chimes of the clock. RICHARD comes in the front door. He wears a sober suit, as in the morning. He puts his briefcase down in the hall and goes into the room. She smiles at him and pours him a whisky.

Hullo.
RICHARD. Hullo.

He kisses her on the cheek. Takes glass, hands her the evening paper and sits down left. She sits on chaise longue with paper.

Thanks.

He drinks, sits back and sighs with contentment.

Aah.
SARAH. Tired?
RICHARD. Just a little.
SARAH. Bad traffic?
RICHARD. No. Quite good traffic, actually.
SARAH. Oh, good.
RICHARD. Very smooth.

Pause.

SARAH. It seemed to me you were just a little late.
RICHARD. Am I?
SARAH. Just a little.
RICHARD. There was a bit of a jam on the bridge.

SARAH gets up, goes to drinks table to collect her glass, sits again on the chaise longue.

Pleasant day?

THE LOVER

SARAH. Mmnn. I was in the village this morning.
RICHARD. Oh yes? See anyone?
SARAH. Not really, no. Had lunch.
RICHARD. In the village?
SARAH. Yes.
RICHARD. Any good?
SARAH. Quite fair. (*She sits.*)
RICHARD. What about this afternoon? Pleasant afternoon?
SARAH. Oh yes. Quite marvellous.
RICHARD. Your lover came, did he?
SARAH. Mmnn. Oh yes.
RICHARD. Did you show him the hollyhocks?

Slight pause.

SARAH. The hollyhocks?
RICHARD. Yes.
SARAH. No, I didn't.
RICHARD. Oh.
SARAH. Should I have done?
RICHARD. No, no. It's simply that I seem to remember your saying he was interested in gardening.
SARAH. Mmnn, yes, he is.

Pause.

Not all that interested, actually.
RICHARD. Ah.

Pause.

Did you go out at all, or did you stay in?
SARAH. We stayed in.
RICHARD. Ah. (*He looks up at the Venetian blinds.*) That blind hasn't been put up properly.
SARAH. Yes, it is a bit crooked, isn't it?

Pause.

EXERCISES:

1. Analyse the text in terms of its diatypic varieties.

2. Rewrite the dialogue, changing the field of discourse to something more compatible with the given personal and functional tenors.

Most of this text was spoken by the auctioneer, and there is a temptation to call it spoken spontaneous monologue. It is clearly, however, attempting to elicit a response (in this case, nonlanguage hand signals).

The text is also, in places, nonspontaneous. Although it is not completely fixed in form, like schoolyard rhymes, portions of the patter of the auctioneer come very close to the mode spoken nonspontaneous reciting.

all right there we have a (laughter) . . . well theres the right word
now (er telescope) telescope is it (uhuh) (yeah) I dont know what
power it is do you know (no) (spyglass) (two power lenses) (spyglass)
ths two power lenses (spyglass) (spyglass) (spyglass) o.k. th spyglass an case an
all an whada ya say on it whod give me ten dollars for it (fingst?) o.k.   5
five an start it (uhuh) fivedollars five thank you is that a fives the bid
an six now at five six dollar dyou wanit at six we'll get six for it at
five an six dollars we're sellin the spyglass (that my bid) yes sir six
an now youre out sir do you wanit at seven seven and eight eight an
nine at eight give nine dollars do you wanidadnine willya give nine   10
for it youre out sir dyou wanit and nine dollars nine eights the bid
nine dollars nine all done at eight dollars nine for it nines the bid ten
at nine an ten now dyou wanit at ten will you give for it at nine give
ten dollars at nine an ten an all done at nine ten for it (heres the bid
right here) where are we thank you mam tenand eleven eleven an   15
twelve twelve an thirteen at twelve give thirteen dollars for it twelve
dollars right here thank you.

EXERCISE:

Discuss the grammar of those portions of the text which most strongly invite response, and show how the mode is related to the functional tenor persuasion.

Part Three

Dialectal Varieties

— Temporal Dialect
— Geographical Dialect
— Social Dialect
— Idiolect

TEMPORAL DIALECT

The *diatypic* varieties, field, mode, personal tenor, and functional tenor, offer the user a range of choice. He can select any field of discourse, speak or write, be formal or informal, persuade, amuse, instruct or abuse, as the situation and his own inclination move him.

There is another range of variety, *dialectal* variety, which offers the user very little choice.

Of the four dialectal varieties (temporal dialect, geographical dialect, social dialect and idiolect) temporal dialect illustrates clearly this lack of choice.

Shakespeare was born in one age and spoke and wrote its dialect; we speak and write another. However, modern speakers and writers, in certain situations, can use temporal dialects earlier than their own. Public prayer, especially those varieties which incorporate passages from the King James Version of the *Bible*, is linguistically conservative. Poets, writers of fiction, and dramatists sometimes attempt to imitate the language patterns of a previous age. Signs of the "Ye Olde Tea Shoppe" variety achieve the same effect at the graphological level.

For the most part, however, we speak and write in the temporal dialect of the period in which we live.

Temporal dialect may be analysed to a very delicate degree. At the lexical level, this passage from Tom Wolfe is marked as later than 1960. "Head", although a familiar word, collocates in this text with "life", "costume", "be-in", "named", and "high-loving", and has clearly become a new lexical item.

EXERCISES:

1. Discuss the way in which two other lexical items in this text have been redefined by their collocation.

2. In a dictionary you are familiar with, find the entries for "head" and the two lexical items from Exercise 1. Discuss the usefulness of the dictionary as a tool for understanding contemporary English.

---

10   TOM WOLFE

bail with the San Mateo County court. I suppose the cours figured they had Kesey either way. If he jumped bail now, it would be such a dirty trick on his friends, costing them their homes, that Kesey would be discredited as a drug apostle or anything else. If he didn't, he would be obliged to give his talk to The Youth—and so much the better. In any case, Kesey was coming out.   5

This script was not very popular in Haight-Ashbury, however. I soon found out that the head life in San Francisco was already such a big thing that Kesey's return and his acid graduation plan were causing the first big political crisis. All eyes were on Kesey and his group known as the   10 Merry Pranksters. Thousands of kids were moving into San Francisco for a life based on LSD and the psychedelic thing. Thing was the major abstract word in Haight-Ashbury. It could mean anything, isms, life styles, habits, leanings, causes, sexual organs; thing and freak; freak referred to styles and ob-   15 sessions, as in "Stewart Brand is an Indian freak" or "the zodiac —that's her freak," or just to heads in costume. It wasn't a negative word. Anyway, just a couple of weeks before, the heads had held their first big "be-in" in Golden Gate Park, at the foot of the hill leading up into Haight-Ashbury, in   20 mock observance of the day LSD became illegal in California. This was a gathering of all the tribes, all the communal groups. All the freaks came and did their thing. A head named Michael Bowen started it, and thousands of them piled in, in high costume, ringing bells, chanting, dancing ecstatic- ally, blowing their minds one way and another and making their favorite satiric gestures to the cops, handing them   30 flowers, burying the bastids in tender fruity petals of love. Oh christ, Tom, the thing was fantastic, a freaking mind- blower, thousands of high-loving heads out there messing up the minds of the cops and everybody else in a fiesta of love and euphoria. Even Kesey, who was still on the run then, had   35 brazened on in and mingled with the crowd for a while, and they were all one, even Kesey—and now all of a sudden here he is, in the hands of the FBI and other supercops, the biggest name in The Life, Kesey, announcing that it is time to "graduate from acid." And what the hell is this, a copout or   40 what? The Stop Kesey movement was beginning even within the hip world.

HEAD

This text is a facsimile reproduction from the only surviving manuscript of the epic poem *Beowulf*. The poem itself was composed in the eighth century, but the manuscript dates from the tenth. The temporal dialect is Old English.

EXERCISES:

1. The text is unmistakably marked at the graphological level. Select the letters in the first five lines which are not in use today.

2. Look at the printed version of the manuscript on the next page. Find, and list, the grammatical and lexical items which are common to both Old English and your own temporal dialect.

p. 1 = fol. 129ᵛ = ll. 1—21.

HWÆT WE GARDE-
na. in¦gear-dagum. þeod-cyninga
þrym ge-frunon hu¦ða æþelingas ellen
fremedon. Oft scyld sceing sceaþena
þreatum *monegum mægþum meodo-setla   5
of-teah egsode eorl syððan ærest wearð
fea-sceaft funden he þæs frofre gebad
weox under wolcnum weorð-myndum þah.
oð þæt him æghwylc þara ymb-sittendr:
*ofer hron-rade hyran scolde gomban   10
gyldan þæt wæs god cyning. ðæm eafera wæs
æfter cenned geong in geardum þone god
sende folce to¦frofre fyren-ðearfe on-
geat *þ hie ær drugon aldor-[le]ase. lange
hwile him þæs lif-frea wuldres wealdend   15
worold-are for-geaf. beowulf wæs breme
blæd wide sprang scyldes eafera scede-
landum in. *Swa sceal [geong g]uma gode
ge-wyrcean fromum feoh-giftum. on¦fæder

[1] The upper part of *E* in *GARDE* gone; *E* A, *e* (as well as the preceding
D) with a different ink B, *e* W.
[2] *ellen* ABW; now the second stroke of *n* gone.
[3] *sceaþena* W, *sceaþen* AB as well as the MS. now.
[4] the blot over, *f* in *of* recent ¦ *feared* over *egsode* in a 16th century hand ¦
wearð A,W, *weard* B; now the whole of *ð* all but gone, only the very top of
it being left.
[5] *gebad* (*d* added with a different ink B) ABW; now *d* gone (no accent
on the *a*).
[6] a letter erased between *hron* and *rade*.
[7] *þ* generally means *þæt*, but sometimes, it would seem, *þa*; cf. Ælfric's
Grammar, 38, 3; 121, 4; 291, 2. ¦ *aldor . . . ase* W, *aldor . . . ase* (*r* altered
from *n*, the second *a* altered from some other letter, and an erasure before it)
A, *aldor . . . tae* B; before the second *a* in MS. a stroke is still visible, such
as generally connects an *e* with a following *a*.
[8] the second *d* of *wealdend* cut through.
[9] *m* in *breme* cut through between the second stroke and the third.
[10] from six to seven letters illegible between *sceat* and *uma*, and even the
u not quite perfect; . . . . *ma* (*ma* added over the line) A, ...
ma B.
[11, 12] *e* both in *gode* and *fæder* cut through.

Chaucer's *Treatise on the Astrolabe*, a prose work written in the late fourteenth century, (reproduced here in modern type, but with the original spelling), presents less difficulty for the modern reader than does *Beowulf*. Its temporal dialect is Middle English.

Part I

Here begynneth the descripcioun of thin Astralabie.

1. Thyn Astrolabie hath a ring to putten on the thombe of thi right hond in taking the height of thinges. And tak kep, for from henes forthward I wol clepen the heighte of any thing that is taken by the rewle "the altitude", withoute moo wordes.

2. This ryng renneth in a maner toret fast to the moder of thyn Astrelabie in so rown a space that it distourbith not the instrument to hangen after his right centre.

3. The moder of thin Astrelabye is thikkest plate, perced with a large hool, that resceiveth in hir wombe the thynne plates compowned for diverse clymates, and thy reet shapen in manere of a nett or of a webbe of a loppe.

4. This moder is dividid on the bakhalf with

EXERCISES:

1. Look up "kep" (you will find it under "keep"), "clepen", and "toret" in the *Oxford English Dictionary*. If available, consult also a dictionary of Middle English and a concordance to the works of Chaucer. Then try rewriting paragraphs 1 and 2 in present-day English.

2. Although some of the verb forms are unfamiliar, the clause structure of this work is recognizable to the modern reader. Describe the grammar of the first two sentences.

This example of early seventeenth-century handwriting is from a manuscript of Shakespeare's *Henry IV, Part I*.

EXERCISE:

Read this text, using the printed version on the next page whenever you have trouble making out a word. In addition to the circled letters, list other graphological features which mark the text as belonging to an earlier temporal dialect than your own.

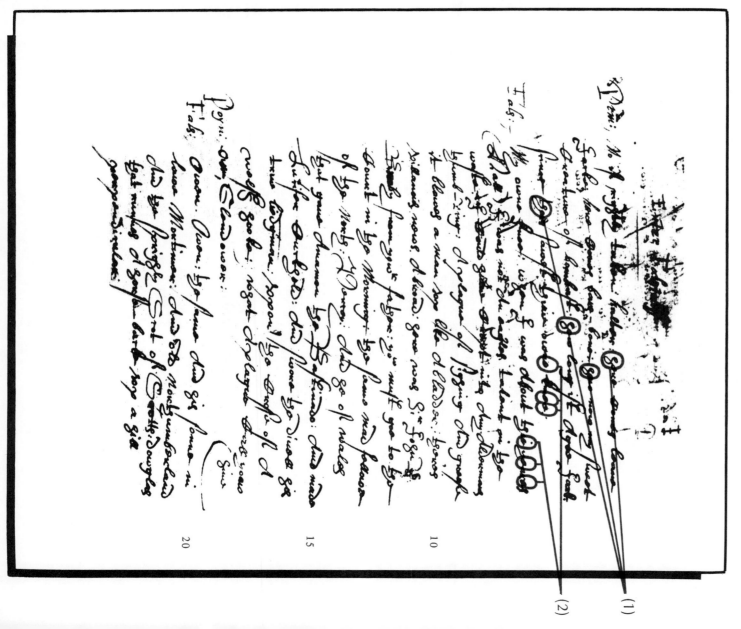

39 WILLIAM SHAKESPEARE
HENRY IV, PART 1, II.iv.328–349 [COPIED CA. 1622]

The passage is extracted from a manuscript version of the two parts of the play, cut and combined into one play, for private performance at Surrenden, Kent, the seat of Sir Edward Dering, bart., by amateur actors. It is the earliest surviving manuscript of any of Shakespeare's plays. The hand is, except for stage-directions and speakers' names, pure secretary. The punctuation, though eccen-

tric and somewhat erratic, is not senseless. Like many other writers of the time, the scribe who copied this dramatic piece uses a form of capital C simply as initial c, and he does the same with capital A. Since these capitals have no significance and since other initials are in the main minuscules, we do not preserve, in the transcript, C and A.

Enter Falstalff.

Prin., No if rightly taken: halter: here comes leane
  Iacke: here comes bare-bone: how now my sweet
  creature of bombast: how long ist agoe Iack:
  scince thow sawest thine owne knee:

Fals.,—My owne knee: when I was about thie yeares   5
  (Hall) I was not an eagles talent in the
  waste: I could haue crept into any aldermans
  thumb-ring: a plague of sighing and greefe
  it blowes a man vp like a bladder: there's   10
  villanous news a broad: here was Sir Iohn (B)
  Braby from yowr father: yow must goe to the
  court in the Morning: the same mad fellowe
  of the North: Percey: and he of wales
  that gaue Amamon the Bastinado: and made   15
  Lucifer cuckhold: and swore the diuell his
  true liedgman: vpon the crosse of a
  welsh hooke: what a plague call yo( )w

Poyn., Owen Glendower: hime

Fals., Owen. Owen: the same and his sonne in   20
  lawe Mortimer: and old Northumberland
  and the sprigh[t]ly Scot of Scotts: dowglas
  that runnes a horse-backe vp a hill
  perpendicular:

104

4 *Iack:*] The trimming of the leaves by a binder appears to have cropped off the upper point of the colon, which on this assumption is here restored.

10 *there's*] Though he misplaced it, we may assume that the writer intended the apos-

trophe to go in the right place. The modern use of the apostrophe in contractions of this sort begins to be met with in the first decades of the seventeenth century.

19 *Owen*] The *w* is written over an *o*.

EXERCISES:

Compare this text, which closely follows the orthography of the manuscript, with an edition of Shakespeare which modernizes spelling and punctuation.

1. List significant differences of the modernized version.

2. At what levels is the modernized version marked as a temporal dialect earlier than your own?

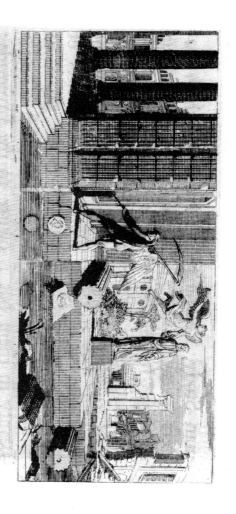

PREFACE.

OMER is universally allow'd to have had the greatest Invention of any Writer whatever. The Praise of Judgment *Virgil* has justly contested with him, and others may have their Pretensions as to particular Excellencies; but his Invention remains yet unrival'd. Nor is it a Wonder if he has ever been acknowledg'd the greatest of Poets, who most excell'd in That which is the very Foundation of Poetry. It is the Invention that in different degrees distinguishes all great Genius's: The utmost Stretch of hu-man

B

5

10

15

P R E F A C E.

man Study, Learning, and Induſtry, which maſters every thing beſides, can never attain to this. It furniſhes Art with all her Materials, and without it Judgment itſelf can at beſt but *ſteal wiſely*: For Art is only like a prudent Steward that lives on managing the Riches of Nature. Whatever Praiſes may be given to Works of Judgment, there is not even a ſingle Beauty in them but is owing to the Invention: [20] As in the moſt regular Gardens, however Art may carry the greateſt Appearance, there is not a Plant or Flower but is the Gift of Nature. The [25] firſt can only reduce the Beauties of the latter into a more obvious Figure, which the common Eye may better take in, and is therefore more entertain'd with. And perhaps the reaſon why [30] moſt Criticks are inclin'd to prefer a judicious and methodical Genius to a great and fruitful one, is, becauſe they find it eaſier for themſelves to purſue their Obſervations through an uniform [35] and bounded Walk of Art, than to comprehend the vaſt and various Extent of Nature.

This text, from the first edition of Alexander Pope's translation of *The Iliad* (1715) is, unlike the *Beowulf* or Chaucer passages, instantly recognizable as Modern English, although we can also see that it is a Modern English earlier than our own.

EXERCISES:

1. Discuss the respects in which the graphology of this text differs from that of the present day.

2. Determine the meaning of the contrasting terms "Invention" and "Judgment" by their collocations in this text, and compare your findings with the appropriate entries in the *Oxford English Dictionary*.

GEOGRAPHICAL DIALECT

All of us speak a dialect, not only of a particular time, but also of a particular place. The British Isles offer an illustration of this. Most people can tell whether a speaker comes from Scotland, England, or Ireland. A person who has an interest in, and a good "ear" for, dialect can tell what *part* of Scotland, for example, a speaker comes from. A fully trained specialist in dialectology can make even finer geographical distinctions.

Within North America, too, there are clearly recognizable dialectal varieties. Southerners, Bostonians, and people from Newfoundland, parts of rural Ontario, and Victoria, B.C. have characteristic speech patterns.

Although geographical dialect is perhaps most obvious on the phonological level, its markers are present in the other levels of speech. At the grammatical level, for example, some geographical dialects of Southern United States speech distinguish between "you" (singular) and "you all" (plural).

Lexis, too, marks geographical dialect: some people might not understand the meaning of "tilt", a lexical item used in the Canadian Maritimes, because their own geographical dialect has instead "seesaw" or "teeter-totter". There are fewer distinctions at the graphological level, but there are some. In Ontario, a driver carries a "licence", unlike his New New York counterpart who must make do with a "license".

The grammar of this passage from *The Children of Sisyphus*, by H. Orlando Patterson, a Jamaican novelist, differs in several respects from ours. The passage opens in the functional tenor narrative. After the first two sentences, the past tense is no longer used, and what appears to be the present tense lacks the terminal "s" by which third-person verbs are distinguished.

> And of course there was the famous Miss Mollypols. One day, sun hot like hell, some Brothers were sitting by the sea mending their net. A little motor-car pull up on the roadside, and what you know? A meagre little woman with thick glasses and two round brown eyes behind them step out. She look to the right. She look to the left. Then she step forward. Not a thing she say. But God, you should see her face. She look like she just see the Holy Ghost. But she still coming forward till she was standing beside the Brethren. She look down at them, but don't say a thing. Every now and then she made as if to speak, but the words them dry up at her throat. All she could do is swallow. Finally Brother Salamanca ask her what business bring her here. She swallow again. She gape. Then at last she say in a voice like a half-dead bird:
>
> 'Good afternoon, gentlemen.'

5

10

15

EXERCISE:

Rewrite the passage in your own geographical dialect, trying to keep other variables (e.g. personal and functional tenor) unchanged.

The passage reproduced below is from a radio script of "Jake and the Kid" by W.O. Mitchell. At the phonological level, the text is marked mainly for social, rather than geographical dialect, as when "Ma" corrects the "Kid's" pronunciation of "Northren". At the lexical level, "wavies", which derives from a Cree word meaning snow geese, clearly marks the geographical dialect as Canadian English.

MA: Sitting, Son.

KID: -- in bed holdin' my breath -- all cold inside my elbows -- Gee, Jake -- like a thousand dogs barkin'!

MA: What were! Look -- if it's a secret you . . . . . .

                                  5

JAKE: Geese. Geese. (WAHT THE AITCH YOU THINK THEY WERE)

MA: Oh. (THAT ALL)

KID: I bet there was five hundred!

JAKE: (Correcting) Mebby fifty, Kid.

KID: Jake -- would they be northren geese?

MA: Northern geese, Son.

                                  10

JAKE: Sure they're Northren geese.

KID: Wavies!

JAKE: (Tinge) Kid -- kid -- you bin raised better'n that.
         Honkers. They was gray. Canada geese. Honkers. ✕

                                                                                    15

MA: The sound of Northern geese coming down is a sad sound.

JAKE: Sound a geese is a real nice . . . Sound

KID: I get a bang out of them!

MA: Frost has blackened the flowers -- there's a sadness --
         end of another year . . . .

                                                                                    20

JAKE: That's right. Harvest's over an' she's time to git out
         the old twelve gauge. ✕

KID: Yeah. (REVERENTLY) Yeah, Oh, Yeah!

MA: (A LITTLE SHORTLY - SHE HAS THINGS ON HER MIND) Son ---
         your porridge.

                                                                                    25

KID: Huh?

EXERCISE:

Description of your own geographical dialect is difficult. Tape record
another geographical dialect, for instance the head of state of another
English-speaking nation on television, or the conversation of a friend from
somewhere else.

Transcribe a portion of the text, and note those details which differ from
your own speech.

EXERCISE:

Many of the words in this poem by Robert Burns are clearly not part of our own temporal and geographical dialects. Try to determine which words are strange because they are Scottish, and which are older forms common to both Scottish and English. In addition to the *Oxford English Dictionary*, you may wish to consult a Scottish dialect dictionary.

58

ROBERT BURNS

And fare thee weel, my only luve!
And fare thee weel a while!
And I will come again, my luve,
Tho' it were ten thousand mile!   5

Ye flowery banks

Ye flowery banks o' bonie Doon,
How can ye blume sae fair?
How can ye chant, ye little birds,
And I sae fu' o' care?   10

Thou'll break my heart, thou bonie bird
That sings upon the bough;
Thou minds me o' the happy days
When my fause luve was true.

Thou'll break my heart, thou bonie bird,   15
That sings beside thy mate;
For sae I sat, and sae I sang,
And wist na o' my fate.

Aft hae I rov'd by bonie Doon,
To see the woodbine twine,   20
And ilka bird sang o' its luve,
And sae did I o' mine.

Wi' lightsome heart I pu'd a rose,
Frae aff its thorny tree;
And my fause luver staw my rose,   25
But left the thorn wi' me.

SOCIAL DIALECT

Often it is difficult to distinguish social dialect from geographical dialect. A given area in a city will have inhabitants who are of a distinct social class. Is the dialect spoken by these people to be called social or geographical?

There is no entirely satisfactory answer to this question, but, to the degree that language features correlate with clearly defined social categories, that variety of language is appropriately termed social dialect. In determining these categories, linguists share the interests of anthropologists and sociologists, and often work in conjunction with them.

Literature often achieves realism by exploiting the differences between social dialects. An accurate transcript of a non-middle-class dialect is here followed by two literary texts written for middle-class audiences but containing imitations of strongly marked social dialects.

The conversation transcribed below is an example of a social dialect which differs from middle-class English.

EXERCISE:

Indicate grammatical and phonological markers of this social dialect.

CONVERSATION 9: what kin' o' work you do

From FC 10-8, recorded 12 September 1966

Speakers: Harry Jones and Michael Jones

MJ: what kìn' o' wórk (do) you dò# (p)

HJ: [ó:w|] (p)

MJ: you bùildin' schóo'# (p)
   constrúction wòrk [kẽtrasẽ wɪ(k)]# (p)   5

HJ: nó# (p) I'm bùildin' a# (p) tés' bùildin'# (p)
   fòr| (p) áirplànes# (p) i's# (p)
   i's prètty good orga'zátion but a# (p)
   lòt o' wòrk [n]# (p)
   tàkes smárt mèns put it úp# (p)   10
   which I'm nòt óne# (p)

MJ: (LAUGHS) do you stáy thère whère you wòrk at|
   for lúnch# (p)   15

HJ: [ʔm̩ʔm|] (p)

MJ: I thòught you gò on pláce| to èat lúnch# (p)

HJ: [ʔm̩ʔm] I stay rìght on jób dòugh# (p)

MJ: [ɑ:m̩#] (p) [ʔɑʔɑʔɑ́:#] (p) whàt you méa- [ɑ:#] (p)   20
   dàt dèy bùildin' on ne pláce# (p)
   an| (p) tánkin' òn ne gróun'# (p)
   òr what éver you càll i'# (p)

CHAPTER I

You don't know about me, without you have read a book by
the name of *The Adventures of Tom Sawyer*, but that ain't
no matter. That book was made by Mr. Mark Twain, and he
told the truth, mainly. There was things which he stretched,
but mainly he told the truth. That is nothing. I never seen   5
anybody but lied, one time or another, without it was Aunt
Polly, or the widow, or maybe Mary. Aunt Polly—Tom's
Aunt Polly, she is—and Mary, and the Widow Douglas, is all
told about in that book—which is mostly a true book; with
some stretchers, as I said before.   10

Now the way that the book winds up, is this: Tom and me
found the money that the robbers hid in the cave, and it made
us rich. We got six thousand dollars apiece—all gold. It
was an awful sight of money when it was piled up. Well,
Judge Thatcher, he took it and put it out at interest, and it   15
fetched us a dollar a day apiece, all the year round—more
than a body could tell what to do with. The Widow Douglas,
she took me for her son, and allowed she would civilize me;
but it was rough living in the house all the time, considering
how dismal regular and decent the widow was in all her ways;   20
and so when I couldn't stand it no longer, I lit out. I got into
my old rags and my sugar-hogshead again, and was free and
satisfied. But Tom Sawyer he hunted me up and said he was
going to start a band of robbers, and I might join if I would go
back to the widow and be respectable. So I went back.   25

The widow she cried over me, and called me a poor lost lamb,
and she called me a lot of other names, too, but she never
meant no harm by it. She put me in them new clothes again,
and I couldn't do nothing but sweat and sweat, and feel all
cramped up. Well, then, the old thing commenced again.   30
The widow rung a bell for supper, and you had to come to time.
When you got to the table you couldn't go right to eating, but
you had to wait for the widow to tuck down her head and
grumble a little over the victuals, though there warn't really   35

185

EXERCISE:

At the grammatical and lexical levels, discuss social dialect in this passage
from the opening chapter of *The Adventures of Huckleberry Finn*.

PYGMALION

HIGGINS [*wounded in his tenderest point by her insensibility to his elocution*] Oh, indeed! I'm mad, am I? Very well, Mrs Pearce: you neednt order the new clothes for her. Throw her out.

LIZA [*whimpering*] Nah-ow. You got no right to touch me.   5

MRS PEARCE. You see now what comes of being saucy. [*Indicating the door*] This way, please.

LIZA [*almost in tears*] I didnt want no clothes. I wouldnt have taken them [*she throws away the handkerchief*]. I can buy my own clothes.   10

HIGGINS [*deftly retrieving the handkerchief and intercepting her on her reluctant way to the door*] Youre an ungrateful wicked girl. This is my return for offering to take you out of the gutter and dress you beautifully and make a lady of you.

MRS PEARCE. Stop, Mr Higgins. I wont allow it. It's you that   15
are wicked. Go home to your parents, girl; and tell them to take better care of you.

LIZA. I aint got no parents. They told me I was big enough to earn my own living and turned me out.

MRS PEARCE. Wheres your mother?   20

LIZA. I aint got no mother. Her that turned me out was my sixth stepmother. But I done without them. And I'm a good girl, I am.

HIGGINS. Very well, then, what on earth is all this fuss about? The girl doesnt belong to anybody—is no use to anybody but   25
me. [*He goes to Mrs Pearce and begins coaxing*]. You can adopt her, Mrs Pearce: I'm sure a daughter would be a great amusement to you. Now dont make any more fuss. Take her downstairs; and—

MRS PEARCE. But whats to become of her? Is she to be paid   30
anything? Do be sensible, sir.

HIGGINS. Oh, pay her whatever is necessary: put it down in the housekeeping book. [*Impatiently*] What on earth will she want with money? She'll have her food and her clothes. She'll only drink if you give her money.

LIZA [*turning on him*] Oh you are a brute. It's a lie: nobody ever saw the sign of liquor on me. [*To Pickering*] Oh, sir; youre   35

EXERCISES:

1. Give the markers of social dialect in Liza's speech.

2. In literature, an author is not always consistent in reproducing a social dialect. Which of Liza's sentences are not marked for her social dialect?

IDIOLECT

Each speaker speaks the language of his time, place, and social background — but he also speaks a language which expresses his individuality. This is called his idiolect. Idiolect is most clearly seen in terms of phonology: the particular nature of his vocal tract, as well as his patterns of articulation, give each speaker a pronunciation which is clearly his own. Few would fail to recognize the voices of John Diefenbaker, Pierre Trudeau, John F. Kennedy or their own parents.

Idiolect is clearly marked graphologically in terms of handwriting. It is also marked by spellings, contractions, and other features which can be printed. Patterns of grammar and lexis, too, mark idiolect in both spoken and written language.

If we exclude handwriting, graphology does not usually provide a very clear indication of an idiolect. These two letters written by Ezra Pound show a strongly individualistic graphological style, even in printed form.

EXERCISE:

In the above text, indicate idiolectal markers at all four levels.

1 9 2 5

203: To James Joyce

Siracusa, 21 January

Can't make out whether Jean de Gourmont wants to translate it or wants ME (porca santa) to trad. In any case as he is a gentleman, send him a line. His firm ought to do *Dubliners*. Also *you* might smoke 'em up to start the series of continental editions of contemporary English books—before Berlin does.

P.S. J. d. G.'s address is 71 rue des Sts. Péres, in case his handschrift is more illegible than mine.

204: To William Bird

Palermo, 25 January

Dear Bill: Bozze recd. Complimenti. *Much* finer than I had expected. Also various things of Henry's look O.K. in double page [drawing] that I had disliked in single [drawing].

He has the larfff on us for p. 16 [drawing] because it wd' have good better the way he meant, only we fergottt abaht the "C", on the next page.

Vurry noble work. And up to date *no* misprint of any importance—only an *i* for an *o* at the end of Piccinini, where it don't matter a cuss. Mos' remarkable. Even the subject matter don't seem so objectionable.

II. Have you a spare page 31 (Canto IX)? Preferably with red. It don't matter about the type. I shd. like to send that sheet to the ole archivista at Ravenna who made me the sketch of the ox-carts. Don't think he reads English. Want enough of page to show him it is part of a book, not a detached picture. Can be sent folded once from top to bottom, but not up the perpendicular middle of page. Not matter of life and death. But if there is a spare slip of that page, on the top arf, can you send it?

III.—/—/Am *much* more pleased than I Xpected to be. And satisfied with Strater where I had before been worried abaht his effex.

Engkore mes compleemengs.

Also size of bok. is pleasant. Can be held on lap, not too heavy, and type read at that distance. A bhloody ghood job. After awl yr. night sweats.

Placuit occulis.

Following is an account, by Edith Wharton, of Henry James rather unsuccessfully asking directions. Mrs. Wharton herself draws attention to a few of the lexical items of which James was overfond.

2 "My good man, if you'll be good enough to come here, please; a little nearer—so," and as the old man came up: "My friend, to put it to you in two words, this lady and I have just arrived here from *Slough*; that is to say, to be more strictly accurate, we have recently *passed through* Slough on our way here, having actually motored to Windsor from Rye, which was our point of departure; and the darkness having overtaken us, we should be much obliged if you would tell us where we are now in relation, say, to the High Street, which, as you of course know, leads to the Castle, after leaving on the left hand the turn down to the railway station." [5]

'I was not surprised to have this extraordinary appeal met by silence, and a dazed expression on the old wrinkled face at the window; nor to have James go on: "In short" (his invariable prelude to a fresh series of explanatory ramifications), "in short, my good man, what I want to put to you in a word is this: supposing we have already (as I have reason to think we have) driven past the turn down to the railway station (which, in that case, by the way, would probably not have been on our left hand, but on our right), where are we now in relation to..." [10] [15]

"'Oh, please," I interrupted, feeling myself utterly unable to sit through another parenthesis, "do ask him where the King's Road is."

"'Ah—? The King's Road? Just so! Quite right! Can you, as a matter of fact, my good man, tell us where in relation to our present position the King's Road exactly *is*?" [20]

"'Ye're in it,' said the aged face at the window.'

167

EXERCISE:

What is distinctive about the grammar James employs in this conversation?

Parody imitates (often with exaggeration) the most striking features of a writer's, or speaker's, idiolect. "Another Book to Cross Off Your List" is a parody of the literary style of the noted critic, F.R. Leavis. It is followed by two samples from Dr. Leavis's own criticism.

EXERCISES:

1. Show how the parody of Dr. Leavis's style in the "Simon Lacerous" passage is based on idiolectal features recognizable in the Sample One text. (Use as a point of departure the circled grammatical and lexical items on pages 168 and 169.)

2. In what ways does the parody more closely resemble Sample Two?

Another Book to Cross Off Your List

BY
SIMON LACEROUS

THE great English novels are *Sons and Lovers*, *Lady Chatterley's Lover*, and *Women in Love*. Some malicious persons, who have had the cheek to call me narrow-minded in the past, will doubtless welcome this statement as proof of their views. I don't care; I let it stick. There will always be literary scum to laugh at every honest effort to make tasteful discriminations, and we are now in greater need than ever before of critics—or shall I say, of *a* critic—who will stand up as a moral and aesthetic guide, leading the culture-hungry masses to the finest and purest literature and keeping the rest in outer darkness. If destiny must choose me as its messenger, I do not shirk from the call, but cry out in all directions: Beware, you complacent dolts who are still wallowing in Victorian trash! Beware, you academic leeches who will

5

10

15

praise any dull sonnet you can find that has not already been worked over by your brethren! A judgment day is at hand! You are going to have to submit your crack-pot notions and juvenile tastes to the severe gaze of common sense, intelligence, and Life!

D. H. Lawrence is the only English novelist worth reading. Now, I know that some of you—the sort that creep around in libraries looking for inconsistencies in a man's work—will say that my position has changed since last year, when I said the great English novelists were Richardson, Fanny Burney, Disraeli, and Lawrence. What you don't seem to realize is that in the meantime another book on the English novel has appeared, by Lord Wendell Dovetail. Now, Lord Wendell Dovetail is a fine person, I suppose; at least he has many friends in his circle, so I am told by some friends of mine who have some contacts in his circle (that kind of counterspy work is not for me, by the bye). I have nothing against Lord Wendell Dovetail personally. But really, I cannot be expected to keep my temper when he publishes a book saying that the great English novelists are Richardson, Fanny Burney, and Disraeli! I went out at once and reread these people, and so did Trixie, and we agreed that they were no good at all.

Now that I have gotten down to Lawrence alone, the number of English novelists on my Index is greater than ever, and this I take to be a sign that things may be im-proving at last on the literary scene. Perhaps readers are finally beginning to learn that their reading time is pre-cious and very limited, and mustn't be wasted on third-raters like Fielding and Joyce.[1] There was an under-

[1] Naturally, there are still persons willing to read into *Tom Jones* a few pages and then pretend to have devoured all of Fiel-

the obvious fact that, though in all this the initiative and drive of
Lawrence's genius must have counted enormously, the initiative
and drive could neither have been what they were, nor could they
have worked to such effect, if there hadn't been conditions other
than personal genius, or 'the individual talent', favouring. To
examine these conditions adequately would be to go into a large
part of English social and cultural history.

It must be enough here to say that the religion of Lawrence's
mother does not deserve the contempt with which Mr Eliot dis-
misses it. The Chapel, in the Lawrence circle, was the centre of a
strong social life, and the focus of a still persistent cultural tradition
that had as its main drive the religious tradition of which Mr Eliot
is so contemptuous. To turn, as Lawrence did, the earnestness and
moral seriousness of that tradition to the powering of a strenuous
intellectual inquiringness was all in the tradition. That the Lawrences
were Congregationalists is a relevant point—their Nonconformity
was very far from being the debased tin-chapel salvationism that
Mr Eliot appears to think it. Congregationalism had a peculiarly
strong intellectual tradition—in what ways does Mr Eliot think
Unitarianism superior? As for the part played by Nonconformity
in English civilization, I suggest that he reads Halévy, though books
alone will not cure that kind of ignorance.

And for those young people in the eighteen-nineties their intellectual education was intimately bound up with a social training,
which, even if it didn't give them Wykehamist or Etonian or even
Harvard manners, I see no reason for supposing inferior to that
enjoyed by Mr Eliot. Moreover, they met and talked and read in a
setting of family life such as, to judge from *The Cocktail Party*, Mr
Eliot cannot imagine to have existed—a family life beset by poverty
and the day-to-day exigencies of breadwinning, yet quite finely
civilized. And further, with what advantageous consequences for
English literature I have pointed out in some detail, Lawrence knew
every day of his life in intimate experience the confrontation, the
interpenetration, of the old agricultural England with the industrial; the contrast of the organic forms and rhythms and the old
beauty of humane adaptation with what had supervened.

As for the intellectual training, *that* Lawrence, I have insisted, did
not lack (and Fr. Tiverton says that he has to agree with me here
as against Mr Eliot). Lawrence, we know was not denied acquain-
tance with formal academic standards. He says some severe things

about Nottingham University College, but he was qualified to make incomparable use of his opportunities, and that he made good use, in formal study, and in informal intercourse intellectual and social, with his friends, we know. In short, I cannot see on what grounds Mr Eliot could assume it to be obvious (if he does—and I don't know what else his tone means) that he himself at twenty-one was better trained intellectually than Lawrence at the same age. He was certainly more sophisticated, and his ability, years older, to proclaim himself, ceremonially, Anglo-Catholic, Royalist, and Classicist, suggests to me that he was certainly less (mature).

I have already made my comment on Mr Eliot's ignorance of the English cultural history, of the English civilization, that is illuminated in E. T.'s Memoir of D. H. Lawrence. It will not be found surprising if I sum up on this head of Lawrence's 'ignorance' by saying that to take him as an example of 'the crippling effect upon men of letters of not having been brought up in the environment of a living and central tradition' seems to me nothing more respectable than an astonishing feat of prejudice—and ignorance.

That Lawrence *was* brought up in a living and central tradition— there, it seems to me, is where to lay the stress. And it seems to me the right answer to the less bluntly repellable form in which Mr Eliot brings his charge in this recent Foreword: 'for Lawrence was an ignorant man in the sense that he was unaware of how much he did not know'. Mr Eliot imputes in particular some defects of knowledge about religion and theology, and (cannot forbear concluding this matter of ignorance with a direct retort. I am not, then, impressed by any superiority of religious and theological knowledge in a writer capable of exposing what is to me the shocking essential ignorance that characterizes *The Cocktail Party*—ignorance of the possibilities of (life: ignorance of the effect the play must have on a kind of reader or spectator of whose existence the author appears to be unaware: the reader who has, himself, found serious work to do in the world and is able to be unaffectedly serious about it, who knows what family life is and has helped to bring up children and who, though capable of being interested in Mr Eliot's poetry, cannot afford cocktail civilization and would reject it, with contempt and boredom, if he *could* afford it.

I come out with these things in order to bring home the force of my insistence that Lawrence *was* brought up in the environment of a living and central tradition. Anything in the nature of *The*

"LAWRENCE SCHOLARSHIP" AND LAWRENCE*

By F. R. LEAVIS

I have tried, but I find it impossible to be grateful to Professor Harry T. Moore for what he has "done for Lawrence." The provocation, in the present volumes, to an ungracious and apprehensive stiffening comes at the very outset, on the page after the title page. We read there:

The Editor dedicates this collection of D. H. Lawrence's letters to

Richard Aldington
David Garnett
Laurence Pollinger.

The implicit pretension is ominous, and the more offensively so because of its particular terms. Who is Professor Harry T. Moore, one asks, and what standing does he suppose he has in relation to the genius of whom he has taken academic possession, that he should dedicate a collection of Lawrence's letters? Had he dedicated it to Aldous Huxley, that indeed one would have acclaimed as an appropriate and graceful gesture. Mr. Huxley's volume was an act of personal judgment and self-committal, and, taking effect as it did a couple of years after Lawrence's death, at a time when it was possible for the distinguished editor of the *Criterion* to judge him not worth an obituary notice, it has an important place in the history of Lawrence's reputation. But Professor Moore takes over Lawrence as an established classic on whom he has been able to consolidate his own position as an "authority" with immediate academic credit and munificent institutional support. And we are contemplating a familiar kind of irony when we reflect that no one at all intelligent about what

*Harry T. Moore (ed.), *The Collected Letters of D. H. Lawrence*, New York (Viking Press), 1962, 2 vols, 1307 pages, $17.50.

makes Lawrence truly a classic and a writer worth devoted study could have put that dedication in front of a body of intimate Laurentian texts.

Laurence Pollinger as a dedicatee one could have passed; there is no significance in a tribute to a literary agent. But the two concerned well-known writers constitute an infelicity so disconcerting that there is much significance in Professor Moore's being unaware of it—as he obviously is. David Garnett's acceptance as a distinguished contemporary writer was a phenomenon of that literary world the nature and power of which were what those who worked for the recognition of Lawrence's genius had most to contend against. Lawrence himself, in one of the letters printed by Professor Moore, mildly calls *Lady into Fox*, the book that established Garnett's fame, "pretty piffle." As for Richard Aldington, Professor Moore tells us under "Who's Who in the Letters": "His most famous novel is *Death of a Hero* (1928)...." In the prose of that work we find chunks of H. G. Wells. It is a familiar case that the author, a scholarly critic with a classical culture, should feel himself a sure judge of form, and be capable, in a contribution to the Nehls "composite biography," of telling us that Lawrence "worked too carelessly and his lack of form was sometimes an exasperation."

The apprehensions started by the dedication are confirmed by the Introduction, where it is borne in on one how lamentably an industrious scholar, specializing in a great creative genius, may be unaware of his own limitations and misconceive his place in the scheme of things. Professor Moore's limitations are such that he should have been particularly careful not to offer anything not strictly required of him as scholar-editor of the texts he has collected and arranged. But one has no sooner said this than one has to recognize that, in the nature of the case, the discrimination is itself beyond him: he has no criterion. And, in a disabling way of which he has no suspicion, he is a complete foreigner in

Part Four

Literature

"Darl" (*As I Lay Dying*, William Faulkner)

Although the categories you have been studying can be extremely useful in the examination of a literary text, it is rare for all of them to be relevant in any one instance. In "Darl", an examination of functional tenor and mode shows how he achieves his stylistic effects.

Written non-fictional narrative is generally past tense, as in a history book. Spoken non-fictional narrative may be past tense or present tense (as in a sports broadcast). When it is in the present tense, spoken narrative generally employs "ing" form verbs, since the action narrated is normally continuing at the time of the narration.

Literature presents a special case. Faulkner has created a "mask"; the passage has the effect of present-tense narration by his character Darl. The language of the passage is not, however, the language that Darl would use if he were addressing us directly in real life; it is, rather, past-tense, written narrative with the verbs in the present.

EXERCISES:

1. Rewrite the Darl passage, changing the appropriate verbs to past tense, so that it becomes normal written narrative. (Imagine, for instance, that you are Darl, making a diary entry later that evening.)

2. By using "ing" form verbs where appropriate, and making any other necessary changes, rewrite the passage as a transcript of Darl's spoken spontaneous monologue. (Imagine that Darl is describing the scene on the telephone. There are, of course, features of the passage which will interfere with the complete achievement of this effect.)

3. Rewrite the passage in the mode written to be read as thought. (Imagine that you are Darl, and that all this is happening before you.)

(149)

Darl

Cash lies on his back on the earth, his head raised on a rolled garment. His eyes are closed, his face is gray, his hair plastered in a smooth smear across his forehead as though done with a paint brush. His face appears sunken a little, sagging from the bony ridges of eye sockets, nose, gums, as though the wetting had slacked the firmness which had held the skin full; his teeth, set in pale gums, are parted a little as if he had been laughing quietly. He lies pole-thin in his wet clothes, a little pool of vomit at his head and a thread of it running from the corner of his mouth and down his cheek where he couldn't turn his head quick or far enough, until Dewey Dell stoops and wipes it away with the hem of her dress.

150   (As I Lay Dying)

Jewel approaches. He has the plane. "Vernon just found the square," he says. He looks down at Cash, dripping too. "Aint he talked none yet?"

"He had his saw and hammer and chalk-line and rule," I say. "I know that."

Jewel lays the square down. Pa watches him. "They cant be far away," pa says. "It all went together. Was there ere a such misfortunate man."

Jewel does not look at pa. "You better call Vardaman back here," he says. He looks at Cash. Then he turns and goes away. "Get him to talk soon as he can," he says, "so he can tell us what else there was."

We return to the river. The wagon is hauled clear, the wheels chocked (carefully; we all helped; it is as though upon the shabby, familiar, inert shape of the wagon there lingered somehow, latent yet still immediate, that violence which had slain the mules that drew it not an hour since) above the edge of the flood. In the wagon bed it lies profoundly, the long pale planks hushed a little with wetting yet still yellow, like gold seen through water, save for two long muddy smears. We pass it and go on to the bank.

One end of the rope is made fast to a tree. At the edge of the stream, knee-deep, Vardaman stands, bent forward a little, watching Vernon with rapt absorption. He has stopped yelling and he is wet to the armpits. Vernon is at the other end of the rope, shoulder-deep in the river, looking back at Vardaman. "Further back than that," he says. "You git back by the tree and hold the rope for me, so it cant slip."

Vardaman backs along the rope, to the tree, moving blindly, watching Vernon. When we come up he looks at us once, his eyes round and a little dazed.

CHAPTER I

In Chancery

LONDON. Michaelmas Term lately over, and the Lord Chancellor sitting in Lincoln's Inn Hall. Implacable November weather. As much mud in the streets, as if the waters had but newly retired from the face of the earth, and it would not be wonderful to meet a Megalosaurus, forty feet long or so, waddling like an elephantine lizard up Holborn Hill. Smoke lowering down from chimney-pots, making a soft black drizzle, with flakes of soot in it as big as full-grown snow-flakes—gone into mourning, one might imagine, for the death of the sun. Dogs, undistinguishable in mire. Horses, scarcely better; splashed to their very blinkers. Foot passengers, jostling one another's umbrellas, in a general infection of ill-temper, and losing their foot-hold at street-corners, where tens of thousands of other foot passengers have been slipping and sliding since the day broke (if this day ever broke), adding new deposits to the crust upon crust of mud, sticking at those points tenaciously to the pavement, and accumulating at compound interest.

Fog everywhere. Fog up the river, where it flows among green aits and meadows; fog down the river, where it rolls defiled among the tiers of shipping, and the waterside pollutions of a great (and dirty) city. Fog on the Essex marshes, fog on the Kentish heights. Fog creeping into the cabooses of collier-brigs; fog lying out on the yards, and hovering in the rigging of great ships; fog drooping on the gunwales of barges and small boats. Fog in the eyes and throats of ancient Greenwich pensioners, wheezing by the firesides of their wards; fog in the stem and bowl of the afternoon pipe of the wrathful skipper, down in his close cabin; fog cruelly pinching the toes and fingers of his shivering little 'prentice boy on deck. Chance people on the bridges peeping over the parapets into a nether sky of fog, with fog all round them, as if they were up in a balloon, and hanging in the misty clouds.

Gas looming through the fog in divers places in the streets, much as the sun may, from the spongy fields, be seen to loom by husbandman and ploughboy. Most of the shops lighted two hours before their time—as the gas seems to know, for it has a haggard and unwilling look.

B

5

10

15

20

25

30

35

The first paragraph of "In Chancery" is dominated by "mud", and the second paragraph, by "fog". The "mud" and "fog", which are described vividly and realistically, are also symbolic.

As soon as it is introduced, "mud" is related to the slime of creation. There is a Biblical echo in the phrase "waters . . . but newly retired from the face of the earth", suggesting both the creation and Noah's flood, and these intimations of a remote past are reinforced by the "Megalosaurus".

The primeval mud in which the dinosaur wallows gives way to the dirty mud of everyday experience, which builds up slowly by falling from above: smoke lowers; there is "a soft black drizzle"; and, with an inversion of the usual association of purity and innocence with white, there is black snow — "flakes of soot in it as big as full-grown snowflakes". The symbolic overtones in this description of the muck falling into the streets become even more explicit as Dickens intensifies the funereal lexis. "Black", "mourning", and "death" are all part of the same lexical set.

Dickens next focusses on the oozing, slippery nature of mud, which is evident in "mire", "splashed", "foot-hold", "slipping", and "sliding". With "deposits to the crust upon crust of mud" the lexis becomes more involved. "Deposits" clearly relates to the falling dirt, but it also operates in an economic set which adds to the symbolic overtones the word has been building up. "Deposits" of mud are described as "accumulating at compound interest", thus linking the unattractive associations of "mud" with the institution of banking. Oozing nature, polluting chimneys, and encumbering financial institutions have all become lexically associated in their common attachment to "mud". The difficulty man has in escaping from his condition is suggested by "tenaciously" and "sticking", describing the tendency of the mud, and hence of the institutions, not to let go.

EXERCISES:

1. In the second paragraph, every sentence but the last begins with the word "fog". Show how the meaning of fog changes progressively from a natural phenomenon to something almost viciously human.

2. Discuss a lexical set which is common to both paragraphs.

"The Fabulous Artificer" (*A Portrait of the Artist as a Young Man*, James Joyce)

The lexical and grammatical complexity of this passage is characteristic of James Joyce's style.

Lexical Patterning: some major sets

The "Artist" of this book is Stephen Daedalus. In this passage three lexical sets, an "artificer" set, a "spiritual flight" set, and a "physical flight" set interact. The first two are directly relevant to Daedalus, the legendary Athenian craftsman, and the third relates to the spiritual condition of Stephen as he contemplates his artistic namesake. "Soaring" is a lexical item common to the "spiritual flight" and the "physical flight" sets, and therefore directly links Stephen and Daedalus.

ARTIFICER

as a Young Man   169

the hazewrapped city. Now, at the name of the fabulous artificer, he seemed to hear the noise of dim waves and to see a winged form flying above the waves and slowly climbing the air. What did it mean? Was it a quaint device opening a page of some medieval book of prophecies and symbols, a hawklike man flying sunward above the sea, a prophecy of the end he had been born to serve and had been following through the mists of childhood and boyhood, a symbol of the artist forging anew in his workshop out of the sluggish matter of the earth a new soaring impalpable imperishable being?

His heart trembled; his breath came faster and a wild spirit passed over his limbs as though he were soaring sunward. His heart trembled in an ecstasy of fear and his soul was in flight. His soul was soaring in an air beyond the world and the body he knew was purified in a breath and delivered of incertitude and made radiant and commingled with the element of the spirit. An ecstasy of flight made radiant his eyes and wild his breath and tremulous and wild and radiant his windswept limbs.

—One! Two! . . . Look out!
—O, cripes, I'm drownded!
—One! Two! Three and away!
—Me next! Me next!
—One! . . . Uk!
—Stephaneforos!

His throat ached with a desire to cry aloud, the cry of a hawk or eagle on high, to cry piercingly of his deliverance to the winds. This was the call of life to his soul not the dull gross voice of the world of duties and despair, not the inhuman voice that had called him to the pale service of the altar. An instant of wild flight had delivered him and the cry of triumph which his lips withheld cleft his brain.

—Stephaneforos!

What were they now but cerements shaken from the body of death—the fear he had walked in night and day, the incertitude that had ringed him round, the shame that had

as a Young Man

1 6 9

the hazewrapped city. Now, at the name of the fabulous artificer, he seemed to hear the noise of dim waves and to see a winged form flying above the waves and slowly climbing the air. What did it mean? Was it a quaint device opening a page of some medieval book of prophecies and symbols, a hawklike man flying sunward above the sea, a prophecy of the end he had been born to serve and had been following through the mists of childhood and boyhood a symbol of the artist forging anew in his workshop out of the sluggish matter of the earth a new soaring impalpable imperishable being?

His heart trembled; his breath came faster and a wild spirit passed over his limbs as though he were soaring sunward. His heart trembled in an ecstasy of fear and his soul was in flight. His soul was soaring in an air beyond the world and the body he knew was purified in a breath and delivered of incertitude and made radiant and commingled with the element of the spirit. An ecstasy of flight made radiant his eyes and wild his breath and tremulous and wild and radiant his limbs.

—One! Two! . . . Look out!
—O, Cripes, I'm drowned!
—One! Two! Three and away!
—Me next! Me next!
—One! . . . Uk!
—Stephaneforos!

His throat ached with a desire to cry aloud, the cry of a hawk or eagle on high, to cry piercingly of his deliverance to the winds. This was the call of life to his soul not the dull gross voice of the world of duties and despair, not the inhuman voice that had called him to the pale service of the altar. An instant of wild flight had delivered him and the cry of triumph which his lips withheld cleft his brain.

—Stephaneforos!

What were they now but cerements shaken from the body of death—the fear he had walked in night and day, the incertitude that had ringed him round, the shame that had

ARTIFICER

SPIRITUAL FLIGHT

PHYSICAL FLIGHT

as a Young Man   1 6 9

the hazewrapped city. Now, at the name of the fabulous artificer, he seemed to hear the noise of dim waves and to see a winged form flying above the waves and slowly climbing the air. What did it mean? Was it a quaint device opening a page of some medieval book of prophecies and symbols a hawklike man flying sunward above the sea, a prophecy of the end he had been born to serve and had been following through the mists of childhood and boyhood, a symbol of the artist forging anew in his workshop out of the sluggish matter of the earth a new soaring impalpable imperishable being?

His heart trembled; his breath came faster and a wild spirit passed over his limbs as though he were soaring sunward. His heart trembled in an ecstasy of fear and his soul was in flight. His soul was soaring in an air beyond the world and the body he knew was purified in a breath and delivered of incertitude and made radiant and commingled with the element of the spirit. An ecstasy of flight made radiant his eyes and wild his breath and tremulous and wild and radiant his windswept limbs.

—One! Two! . . . Look out!
—O, cripes, I'm drownded!
—One! Two! Three and away!
—Me next! Me next!
—One! . . . Uk!
—Stephaneforos!

His throat ached with a desire to cry aloud, the cry of a hawk or eagle on high, to cry piercingly of his deliverance to the winds. This was the call of life to his soul not the dull gross voice of the world of duties and despair, not the inhuman voice that had called him to the pale service of the altar. An instant of wild flight had delivered him and the cry of triumph which his lips withheld cleft his brain.

—Stephaneforos!

What were they now but cerements shaken from the body of death—the fear he had walked in night and day, the incertitude that had ringed him round, the shame that had

the hazewrapped city. Now, at the name of the fabulous artificer, he seemed to hear the noise of dim waves and to see a winged form flying above the waves and slowly climbing the air. What did it mean? Was it a quaint device opening a page of some medieval book of prophecies and symbols, a hawklike man flying sunward above the sea, a prophecy of the end he had been born to serve and had been following through the mists of childhood and boyhood, a symbol of the artist forging anew in his workshop out of the sluggish matter of the earth a new soaring impalpable imperishable being?

His heart trembled; his breath came faster and a wild spirit passed over his limbs as though he were soaring sunward. His heart trembled in an ecstasy of fear and his soul was in flight. His soul was soaring in an air beyond the world and the body he knew was purified in a breath and delivered of incertitude and made radiant and commingled with the element of the spirit. An ecstasy of flight made radiant his eyes and wild his breath and tremulous and wild and radiant his windswept limbs.

—One! Two! . . . Look out!
—O, cripes, I'm drownded!
—One! Two! Three and away!
—Me next! Me next!
—One! . . . Uk!
—Stephaneforos!

His throat ached with a desire to cry aloud, the cry of a hawk or eagle on high, to cry piercingly of his deliverance to the winds. This was the call of life to his soul not the dull gross voice of the world of duties and despair, not the inhuman voice that had called him to the pale service of the altar. An instant of wild flight had delivered him and the cry of triumph which his lips withheld cleft his brain.

—Stephaneforos!

What were they now but cerements shaken from the body of death—the fear he had walked in night and day, the incertitude that had ringed him round, the shame that had

The interrelation of grammatical and lexical patterning

The sentence "An ecstasy of flight made radiant his eyes and wild his breath and tremulous and wild and radiant his windswept limbs" reveals, at the clause rank, a balanced series of complements.

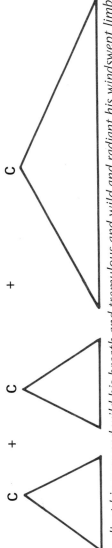

radiant his eyes and wild his breath and tremulous and wild and radiant his windswept limbs

Each complement consists of a rankshifted minor clause in which, despite the lack of a verb, the subject-complement relationship of the two nominal groups is unmistakable.

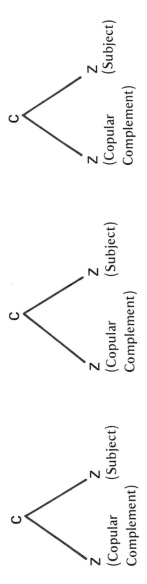

Joyce's balance stands out distinctly because each complement inverts the normal minor clause order which would be "made his eyes radiant and his breath wild and his windswept limbs tremulous and wild and radiant".

Lexis and grammar work here together to emphasize the drawing together of ideas in the Daedalus image. The adjectives distributed through the Z copular complements are symetrically distributed: "radiant", "wild", "tremulous", "wild", and "radiant". "Radiant" in collocation with "eyes" suggests primarily the lexical set of "ecstasy", with a possible secondary suggestion of the bright sunshine involved in the high flight. "Wild" picks up the bird lexis which has come earlier, and which will be emphasized in the next paragraph. It also contrasts with the "constriction" set running through the page: "Hazewrapped" in the first line, "sluggish matter", "gross", "duties", "service", "cerements", "ringed . . . round".

182

Wildness and freedom are linked explicitly to the flight theme in the last, and quite deliberately the most complicated, of the complements: "and tremulous and wild and radiant his windswept limbs."

EXERCISES:

After the "ecstasy of flight" sentence, the mode abruptly shifts and the field appears to be entirely unrelated to the narrative.

1. Show how the grammar and lexis of the dialogue differ from that of the narrative.

2. How does the lexical item "drownded" relate what Stephen hears to his internal experience? (If you are not sure, look up Daedalus and Icarus in a good encyclopaedia or dictionary of mythology.)

3. The lexis of flight continues as Joyce returns to narrative. A new lexical set is, however, introduced. List the items in this "human voice" set, and show how these new collocations express Stephen's discovery of his vocation as a writer.

"My Last Duchess", Robert Browning

"My Last Duchess" is a dramatic monologue. Its mode is written to be read as speech, and the speech which is imitated is in the mode spontaneous monologuing. Browning's attempt to make the speaker sound spontaneous is seen particularly in the grammar of the poem. The clauses, for the most part, follow the normal ordering of spoken language. Subjects precede verbs, and complements and adjuncts follow verbs. Browning's achievement of spontaneity is all the more remarkable because the poem is written in heroic couplets, a form which usually demands extreme syntactic dislocations to meet the requirements of rhyme.

In the analysis of non-literary varieties of English, situation often has an impact on the meaning of a text. In "My Last Duchess", as in literature generally, the situation is created by the poem.

MY LAST DUCHESS   131

My Last Duchess

FERRARA

That's my last Duchess painted on the wall,
Looking as if she were alive. I call
That piece a wonder, now: Frà Pandolf's hands
Worked busily a day, and there she stands.
Will't please you sit and look at her? I said   5
"Frà Pandolf" by design, for never read
Strangers like you that pictured countenance,
The depth and passion of its earnest glance,
But to myself they turned (since none puts by
The curtain I have drawn for you, but I)   10
And seemed as they would ask me, if they durst,
How such a glance came there; so, not the first
Are you to turn and ask thus. Sir, 'twas not
Her husband's presence only, called that spot
Of joy into the Duchess' cheek: perhaps   15
Frà Pandolf chanced to say "Her mantle laps
Over my Lady's wrist too much," or "Paint
Must never hope to reproduce the faint
Half-flush that dies along her throat": such stuff
Was courtesy, she thought, and cause enough   20
For calling up that spot of joy. She had
A heart—how shall I say?—too soon made glad,
Too easily impressed; she liked whate'er
She looked on, and her looks went everywhere.
Sir, 'twas all one! My favour at her breast,   25
The dropping of the daylight in the West,
The bough of cherries some officious fool
Broke in the orchard for her, the white mule   30

132   ROBERT BROWNING

She rode with round the terrace—all and each
Would draw from her alike the approving speech,
Or blush, at least. She thanked men,—good! but
    thanked
Somehow—I know not how—as if she ranked   35
My gift of a nine-hundred-years-old name
With anybody's gift. Who'd stoop to blame
This sort of trifling? Even had you skill
In speech—(which I have not)—to make your will
Quite clear to such an one, and say "Just this   40
Or that in you disgusts me; here you miss,
Or there exceed the mark"—and if she let
Herself be lessoned so, nor plainly set
Her wits to yours, forsooth, and made excuse,
—E'en then would be some stooping, and I choose   45
Never to stoop. Oh, Sir, she smiled, no doubt
Whene'er I passed her; but who passed without
Much the same smile? This grew; I gave commands;
Then all smiles stopped together. There she stands
As if alive. Will't please you rise? We'll meet   50
The company below, then, I repeat,
The Count your master's known munificence
Is ample warrant that no just pretence
Of mine for dowry will be disallowed;
Though his fair daughter's self, as I avowed   55
At starting, is my object. Nay, we'll go
Together down, Sir! Notice Neptune, tho',
Taming a sea-horse, thought a rarity,
Which Claus of Innsbruck cast in bronze for me!   60

EXERCISES:

1. Discuss the grammatical, lexical, and graphological markers of spontaneity in the poem.

2. Discuss the implied situation. What can you tell about the social distinction between the two men?

"nobody loses all the time", e.e. cummings

This narrative poem is written to be read as a spontaneous mono-logue. It consists (with the exception of the first line), of one long sentence, in which the various elements are strung together by a series of "and's". It is also marked as monologue by the interjections, or "fillers", such as "to use a highfalootin phrase", which are scattered throughout the poem.

The functional tenor "amusement" is established by imitation of an outrageously rambling narrative, which consistently violates the assertion of the opening line, "nobody loses all the time", until the statement be-comes suddenly and ironically true at the end of the poem. Amusement also results from the use of stilted and inappropriate language, such as "that is or to wit", language which might in other situations represent a rather inept attempt by a speaker to affect a different social dialect, but which is here a burlesque by the narrator of just such tendencies.

The careful modulation of field of discourse also creates humour. The one-line opening stanza, "nobody loses all the time", establishes a field for the entire poem: failure. The second stanza discusses failure and success; the third seems to abandon the field for a moment, although "indulged" and "inexcusable" are not unrelated to it. The fourth, fifth, and sixth stanzas are concerned with vegetable farm failure, skunk farm failure, and general human failure, followed in the seventh by the most ironic of all — failure to be properly buried. The discussion of "worms" in connection with death is mildly taboo, but in this case the lexical preparation for "worm farm" has been thorough, and results in explosive laughter at the end of the poem.

EXERCISE:

Discuss the personal tenor of this poem. How do markers of formality contribute to its humour?

nobody loses all the time

nobody loses all the time

i had an uncle named
Sol who was a born failure and
nearly everybody said he should have gone
into vaudeville perhaps because my Uncle Sol could
sing McCann He Was A Diver on Xmas Eve like Hell Itself which 5
may or may not account for the fact that my Uncle

Sol indulged in that possibly most inexcusable
of all to use a highfalootin phrase
luxuries that is or to 10
wit farming and be
it needlessly
added

my Uncle Sol's farm
failed because the chickens 15
ate the vegetables so
my Uncle Sol had a
chicken farm till the
skunks ate the chickens when

my Uncle Sol 20
had a skunk farm but
the skunks caught cold and
died and so
my Uncle Sol imitated the
skunks in a subtle manner 25

or by drowning himself in the watertank
but somebody who'd given my Uncle Sol a Victor
Victrola and records while he lived presented to
him upon the auspicious occasion of his decease a 30

E. E. CUMMINGS 67

scrumptious not to mention splendiferous funeral with

tall boys in black gloves and flowers and everything and

i remember we all cried like the Missouri

when my Uncle Sol's coffin lurched because

somebody pressed a button

(and down went

my Uncle

Sol

and started a worm farm)

35

E. E. CUMMINGS *68*

188

Letters to Lord Bute and Lord Chesterfield, Dr. Johnson

The first of these two letters from Dr. Johnson is an honest and serious letter of thanks to a man who was instrumental in securing him royal patronage. The second, the well-known letter to Lord Chesterfield, is highly ironic and insulting. Its irony arises from the discrepancy between the conventionally polite form in which the letter is written and its unmistakably vitriolic content.

The letter to Lord Bute is a conventional eighteenth-century letter to a patron. The functional tenor is essentially phatic, but the establishment of a feeling of good will is coupled with a clear indication of deference and obligation, and, in addition, is generous in its overt praise. The letter to Lord Chesterfield begins with precisely these functional tenors, but shifts rapidly to narrative, blame, and direct expression of hostility. It does this without seriously violating the formal conventions of the letter to a patron, thus giving the letter its cutting thrust of irony.

EXERCISES:

1. Show markers of the functional tenor of the letter to Lord Bute, and of the parallel functional tenor in the letter to Lord Chesterfield.

2. Show markers of other functional tenors in the letter to Lord Chesterfield.

PASSIVE
CONSTRUCTIONS

FLATTERING
LEXIS

BALANCED
STRUCTURE

'To The Right Honourable the Earl of Bute

'My Lord—When the bills were yesterday delivered to me by Mr. Wedderburne, I was informed by him of the future favours which his Majesty has, by your Lordship's recommenda-
tion, been induced to intend for me.

'Bounty always receives part of its value from the manner in which it is bestowed: your Lordship's kindness includes every circumstance that can gratify delicacy, or enforce obligation. You have conferred your favours on a man who has neither alliance nor interest, who has not merited them by services, nor courted them by officiousness; you have spared him the shame of solicita-
tion, and the anxiety of suspense.

'What has been thus elegantly given, will, I hope, not be reproachfully enjoyed; I shall endeavour to give your Lordship the only recompense which generosity desires,—the gratifica-
tion of finding that your benefits are not improperly bestowed.

'I am, my Lord, your Lordship's most obliged, most obedient, and most humble servant,

'Sam. Johnson.'

'July 20, 1762.'

"MY LORD"

TRADITIONAL
ING FORMULA

TO THE RIGHT HONOURABLE THE EARL OF CHESTERFIELD

February 7, 1755.

My Lord

I have been lately informed, by the proprietor of *The World*, that two papers,[1] in which my Dictionary is recommended to the publick, were written by your Lordship. To be so distinguished, is an honour, which, being very little accustomed to favours from the great, I know not well how to receive, or in what terms to acknowledge.

5

10

When, upon some slight encouragement, I first visited your Lordship, I was overpowered, like the rest of mankind, by the enchantment of your address; and could not forbear to wish that I might boast myself *Le vainqueur du vainqueur de la terre;*—that I might obtain that regard for which I saw the world contending; but I found my attendance so little encouraged, that neither pride nor modesty would suffer me to continue it. When I had once addressed your Lordship in publick, I had exhausted all the art of pleasing which a retired and uncourtly scholar can possess. I had done all that I could; and no man is well pleased to have his all neglected, be it ever so little.

15

20

Seven years, my Lord, have now past, since I waited in your outward rooms, or was repulsed from your door; during which time I have been pushing on my work through difficulties, of which it is useless to complain, and have brought it, at last, to the verge of publication, without one act of assistance, one word of encouragement, or one smile of favour. Such treatment I did not expect, for I never had a Patron before.

25

30

The shepherd in Virgil grew at last acquainted with Love, and found him a native of the rocks.[2]

Is not a Patron, my Lord, one who looks with unconcern on a man struggling for life in the water, and, when he has

35

[1] Nos. 100, 101.
[2] *Eclogue,* 8, 11. 43 ff. Johnson borrows his thrust from the pastoral, a form "easy, vulgar, and therefore disgusting."

reached ground, encumbers him with help? The notice which you have been pleased to take of my labours, had it been early, had been kind; but it has been delayed till I am indifferent, and cannot enjoy it; till I am solitary, and cannot impart it; till I am known, and do not want it. I hope it is no very cynical asperity not to confess obligations where no benefit has been received, or to be unwilling that the Publick should consider me as owing that to a Patron, which Providence has enabled me to do for myself.

40

45

Having carried on my work thus far with so little obligation to any favourer of learning, I shall not be disappointed though I should conclude it, if less be possible, with less; for I have been long wakened from that dream of hope, in which I once boasted myself with so much exultation, my Lord,

your Lordship's most humble,

most obedient servant,

SAM: JOHNSON.

50

TO MRS. MONTAGU

Gray's Inn, Dec. 17, 1759.

55

Madam

Goodness so conspicuous as yours will be often solicited, and perhaps sometimes solicited by those who have little pretension to your favour. It is now my turn to introduce a petitioner, but such as I have reason to believe you will think worthy of your notice. Mrs. Ogle, who kept the music-room in Soho Square, a woman who struggles with great industry for the support of eight children, hopes by a benefit concert to set herself free from a few debts, which she cannot otherwise discharge. She has, I know not why, so high an opinion of me as to believe that you will pay less regard to her application than to mine. You know, Madam, I am sure you know, how hard it is to deny, and therefore would not wonder at my compliance, though I were to suppress a motive which you know not, the vanity of being supposed to be of any importance to Mrs. Montagu. But though I may be willing to see

60

65

70

"I Have a Dream", Martin Luther King

Below is an orthographic transcription of the concluding portion of Martin Luther King's speech at the 1963 march on Washington, made from a phonograph record (Mercury SR 61 70). The speech makes use of verbal parallelism and repetition with variation which are often features of formal public speaking.

EXERCISES:

1. Identify each of the four quoted phrases and show how Dr. King weaves these quotations into the fabric of his "sermon".

2. Discuss the grammatical and lexical parallels (some of the most obvious are underlined) which help to establish the functional tenor of persuasion in "I have a dream".

"I have a dream", Martin Luther King, Jr.

I have a dream . . . that one day . . . this nation will rise up . . . an live out the true meaning of its creed . . . "we hold these truths to be self-evident . . . that all men are created equal" (Applause) I have a dream . . . that one day on the red hills of Georgia . . . sons of former slaves and the sons of former slave owners . . . will be able to sit down together at the table of brotherhood . . . I have a dream . . . (Applause) → that one day (Applause) → even the state of Mississippi a state sweltering with the . . . heat of . . . injustice . . . . (Yes) sweltering with the heat of oppression . . . . will be transformed into an oasis of freedom and justice I have a dream . . . . (Applause) that my four little children . . . will one day live in a nation where they will not be judged by the colour of their skin but by the content of their character . . . . I have a dream today (Applause) I have a dream that one day . . . . in Alabama . . . . with its vicious racists . . . . with its governor having his lips dripping with the words of interposition and nullification (Noise) one day right there in Alabama little black boys and black girls . . . . will be able to join hands with little white boys and white girls . . . . as sisters and brothers . . . . I have a dream today (Applause) → I have a dream that one day . . "every valley shall be exalted (Noise) every hill an mountain shall be made low an the rough places will be made plain . . . . an the crooked places will be made straight (Noise) → and the whole glory of the Lord shall be revealed an all flesh shall see it together" (Noise) this is our hope . . . . this is the faith that I go back to the South with . . . . (Yes) with this faith . . . . we will be able to hew out of the mountain of despair . . . . a stone of hope . . . . with this faith . . . . we will be able to transform the jangling discords of our nation . . . . into a beautiful symphony of brotherhood . . . . with this faith we will be able to work together to pray together . . . . to struggle together . . . . to go to jail together . . . . to stand up for freedom together (Applause) → knowing that we will . . . . be free one day (Applause) → it will be the day . . . . it will be the day . . . . when all of God's children (Yes) . . . . will be able to sing with new meaning . . . "my country tis of thee . . . . sweet land of liberty of thee I sing land where my fathers died land of the pilgrims pride . . . . from every . . . . mountainside . . . . let freedom ring" and if America is to be a great nation . . . . this must become true . . . . so let freedom ring . . . . from the prodigious hilltops of New Hampshire . . . . let freedom ring . . . . from the mighty mountains of New York . . . . let freedom ring from the heightening Alleghenies of Pennsylvania . . . . let freedom ring from from the snow-capped Rockies of Colorado . . . . let freedom ring from from the curvacious slopes of California (Applause) → but not only that . . . . let freedom ring from Stone Mountain of Georgia (Applause) → . . . . let freedom ring from . . . . Lookout Mountain of Tennessee (Applause) → . . . let freedom ring from every hill . . . . an molehill of Mississippi (Applause) → from every mountainside (Applause) . . . . let freedom ring

(Applause → inaudible)

when we let it ring from every village an every hamlet . . . . from every state an every city . . . . we will be able to speed up that day . . . when all of God's children . . . . blackmen and whitemen . . . . Jews and Gentiles . . . . Protestants and Catholics . . . . will be able to join hands . . . . and sing in the words of the old negro spiritual . . . . "free at last . . . . free at last (Applause) → thank God almighty we are free at last".

5

10

15

20

25

30

35

40

45

50

Glossary

GLOSSARY

ACCENT: A distinct phonetic and/or phonological pattern characteristic of a geographical area or social class. For example, a British speaker or a southern United States speaker has an accent which is immediately familiar to all of us. (See *Dialect*.)

ADJUNCT: One of the five elements of clause structure. Any element other than subject, predicator, complement or Z is an *adjunct*. The clause "I pulled up the plant very carefully, because it was covered with thorns" contains the easily recognizable subject "I", predicator "pulled", and complement "the plant". The other elements in the clause ("up", "very carefully", and "because it was covered with thorns") are adjuncts. (See *Clause structure*.)

AUXILIARY: An element of verbal group structure. In the clause "She will come on Tuesday", "will come" is a verbal group having "will" as auxiliary in its structure. (See *Group structure*.)

CLAUSE: The unit of English grammar ranked below the sentence and above the group. A clause is typically made up of groups and (by itself or with one or more other clauses) makes up a sentence; for example, in the sentence "my brother hung the picture, and his hammer damaged the wall", there are two *sentence* elements: the clause "my brother hung the picture", and the clause "and his hammer damaged the wall." The clause "and his hammer damaged the wall", is made up of four *clause* elements: an adjunct, "and"; a subject, "his hammer"; a predicator, "damaged"; and a complement, "the wall". Each of these *clause* elements is a group. (See *Rank scale* and note the important exception discussed in *Rankshift*.)

CLAUSE STRUCTURE: The patterning of the five elements in a clause: predicator, subject, complement, Z element and adjunct. The most easily identifiable is the predicator, which is always filled by a verbal group. Other elements are recognized by their relationship to the predicator. In each of the two clauses "John bit the dog", and "the dog bit John", the predicator is "bit"; the subject is the *clause* element which precedes the predicator, and the complement that which follows. Some clauses have no predicator; for instance, "and his brother a hot dog", which occurs as the second *sentence* element in the sentence "He ordered a hamburger and his brother a hot dog". "His brother" and "a hot dog", which do not bear an overt relationship to a predicator, are called Z elements. The "and" which relates the second clause to the first is one type of adjunct.

COLLOCATION: The tendency of lexical items to occur regularly near each other. Some collocations are more probable than others. We would expect "eat" to collocate with "steak" fairly frequently, and almost never to collocate with "cement". Other highly probable items are "tune up" and "engine", "car" and "drive", and "student" and "school".

COMPLEMENT: One of the five elements of clause structure. It is normally a nominal group immediately following the predicator. "The cake" in "She ate the cake", and "a real kitten" in "She's a real kitten" are both complements. The order is sometimes changed for emphasis or other special effects. Note, for example, the complement "One dollar" in "One dollar I might pay, but not two dollars". (See *Clause structure*.)

DELICACY: The degree of detail at which analysis is conducted. For example, at low delicacy "John" and "potatoes" in "John grows potatoes" are both nouns; at higher delicacy, "John" is identified as proper, and "potatoes" as common. Similarly, at low delicacy, speech can be described as either written or spoken. (An Eaton's catalogue and a filmscript are both written.) Analysis at higher delicacy reveals differences (the filmscript, but not the catalogue, is written to be spoken), and at still higher delicacy reveals even more differences (the filmscript, unlike many speeches, is written to be spoken as if not written).

DIALECT: A distinct variety of language characteristic of a geographical area or a social class. Dialect is a broader term than "accent" because it involves distinctions not only of phonetics and/or phonology, but also of grammar and lexis. (See *Accent*.)

DIALECTAL VARIETIES: The four varieties of language over which the user can exert only limited choice: temporal, social and geographical dialects, and idiolect. Temporal dialect provides a clear example. We speak modern English, and not the temporal dialect of Shakespeare. One can, of course, make some changes with effort; an actor, by memorizing the text, can speak with the grammar and lexis of Shakespeare's time, but he can never recapture the phonology, for many details of the pronunciation are unknown. (See *Temporal dialect, Social dialect, Geographical dialect,* and *Idiolect*.)

DIATYPIC VARIETIES: The four varieties of language over which the user can exert more frequent choice: field of discourse, mode of discourse, personal tenor of discourse and functional tenor of discourse. The language user is continually exercising conscious or unconscious choice among these; for example, he will decide whether to give a particular instruction by a written memorandum or a telephone call (mode of discourse). A lawyer may ask a client the same questions in his office and later in court. His language in court will almost certainly be much more formal (personal tenor). (See *Field of discourse, Mode of discourse, Personal tenor* and *Functional tenor*.)

ELEMENT: A constituent in the structure of a unit of English grammar. A clause has a structure of five elements: subject, predicator, complement, Z, and adjunct. (See *Clause structure*.) The nominal group "my car over there" contains three elements: a modifier "my", a head "car", and a qualifier "over there". (See *Group structure*.)

EXPOSITORY: A category of functional tenor. (See *Functional tenor*.)

FIELD OF DISCOURSE: One of the four diatypic varieties. It is roughly equivalent to the subject being discussed. The term is more precise, however, because it involves levels of delicacy. Thus we could speak of the "field" of fishing, which would be marked by lexical items such as "catch", "tuna", etc. At higher levels of delicacy we would distinguish the "fields" of sports fishing, fresh-water sports fishing, fresh-water dry-fly sports fishing, etc. Each level would have its own markers, but would also share markers common to the field at low delicacy. (See *Delicacy, Lexical item,* and *Marker*.)

FIELD RESTRICTED: A lexical item which has acquired a special meaning within a particular field of discourse. For example, the lexical item "eye" has a different field restricted meaning in the fields of sewing, hurricanes, and potato planting. The field restricted meaning is made evident by an item's collocation. "Tree" in collocation with "shoe" has one meaning; in collocation with "apples" it has a different meaning.

FORMAL: (See *Personal tenor*.)

FUNCTIONAL TENOR: One of the four diatypic varieties: language used to achieve a social end. There are many functional tenors, some of the most frequent being phatic, expository, didactic, persuasive, commanding and narrative. For example, "It is a beautiful day", when spoken in a friendly voice helps to establish a personal relationship. The functional tenor in this case is "phatic".

GEOGRAPHICAL DIALECT: A regional variety of language which is marked by lexical, phonological and grammatical features. (See *Dialectal varieties*.)

GLOSS: An explanation of unfamiliar terms (by definition, example, or collocation). These pages are examples of glosses.

GRAMMAR: One of the levels of linguistic description. (Others are *Lexis* and *Phonology*/*Graphology*.) (See *Level*, and pages 11-53.)

GRAPHIC RESOURCES: The means human beings have to communicate with each other through features taken in by the eye. Graphic resources may be organized as language (see *Graphic substance* and *Graphology*) or they may communicate in a non-language way, as in the black band around a formal card of condolence. There are cases, such as the large woodcut initial letters in old books when the distinction between language and non-language use of graphic resources is not clear.

GRAPHIC SUBSTANCE: The letters, punctuation marks, and other symbols in which a written language can be expressed.

GRAPHOLOGY: The study of the patterned way in which graphic substance is related to the grammar and lexis of a language.

GROUP: The unit of English grammar ranked below the clause and above the word. A typical "group" is made up of one or more words, and it makes up clauses. "My mother" in the clause "My mother is coming next Tuesday" is a group. It is made up of two words: "My" and "mother". It is one of the three groups: a nominal group "My mother", a verbal group "is coming", and an adjunctival group "next Tuesday". A group often consists of only one word: for example, the verbal group "came" in "My mother came last Tuesday".

GROUP STRUCTURE: The recognizable pattern which words assume in the unit group. Two frequently occurring groups are *nominal* groups and *verbal* groups. Each has a distinctive structure.

1. *Nominal group*: A group, consisting of one or more words, which can occur as subject or complement in a clause. "He" in "He runs", "I" and "my shirt" in "I iron my shirt", and an "amalgamated circuit breaker type panelboard" in "Buy an amalgamated circuit breaker type panelboard" are all nominal groups. The key structural element in a *nominal* group is the head, The head is easily recognizable. The heads in our examples are "He", "I", "shirt", and "panelboard". Every nominal group must have a head. In addition it may have one or more words before the head. These are called *modifiers*. "My ten old iron golf clubs" has five modifiers: "My", "ten", "old", "iron", and "golf". A nominal group can also have words which follow the head. These are called *qualifiers*. In "the table in the corner" the words "in the corner" form a qualifier. The structure of a nominal group therefore consists of the obligatory element *head* and the optional elements *modifier* and *qualifier*. All modifiers occur before the head, and all qualifiers occur after the head.

2. *Verbal group*: A group consisting of one or more words which can occur as a predicator in a clause. "Run" in "I run" and "may fall" in "she may fall" are verbal groups. Unlike nominal groups, verbal groups do not necessarily have heads. When they do, the head is easily recognized. Both of the above examples have heads: "run" and "fall". Words in the verbal group which occur before the head are *auxiliaries*. "May" in "may fall" is an auxiliary. A verbal group often contains only auxiliaries. "Might" in "He might" and "should have" in "She should have" are examples of predicators consisting of auxiliary elements. The structure of the verbal group

therefore consists of an optional head, and one or more optional auxiliaries. If both head and auxiliary elements occur in a verbal group, the head is always last.

HEAD: An element of group structure. (See *Group structure*.)

IDIOLECT: The language spoken or written by a particular individual. While he shares many language features with others, certain patterns will be his, and his alone. An individual's voice or handwriting are easily recognized idiolectal features. (See *Dialectal varieties*.)

INFORMAL: (See *Personal tenor*.)

ITEM: (See *Lexical item*.)

LEVEL: A distinct kind of patterning. Linguistics considers these levels: graphology/phonology, the patterning of marks/sounds; grammar, the patterning of restricted systems; lexis, the patterning of vocabulary. (The term "level" does not imply that one level is higher than another, only that it is different.) Part One of this book describes levels of language.

LEXICAL ITEM: A word or group of words entering into collocational relationships. For example, "light" and "turn out" in the sentence "She will turn out the light". Other lexical items apt to collocate with "turn out" are "dark" and "lamp". Note that the lexical item "turn out" consists of more than one word. (See *Collocation* and *Lexical set*.)

LEXICAL SET: Any number of lexical items that tend to occur near each other or near a common item. A set is an "open" pattern, in contrast to the "closed" systems characteristic of grammar. Its open nature permits potentially unlimited numbers of collocating items. (See *Collocation*.) In the sentence "I would rather <u>drink</u> two <u>glasses</u> of <u>milk</u> than one <u>bottle</u> of <u>ginger ale</u>", the classes of the words underlined (one verb and four nouns) are dictated by the closed system of grammar, but the actual items that appear are selected from the open set of collocating items centred on the common item *drink*.

LEXIS: A level of linguistic description concerned with certain language choices which are not part of the grammatical system. The choice between "man", "dog", and "cow" in "He killed the ——" is lexical; the choice between "man" and "men", "dog" and "dogs", "cow" and "cows" is grammatical, because it operates within the fixed grammatical number system of singular and plural. (See *Level* and *Lexical set*.)

MARKER: A formal feature on any level of language description which occurs regularly in a particular variety. The lexical item "petrol" is a marker of British English; quotation marks and clause patterns similar to those of spoken language mark the mode written to be read as speech: "Mary", she said, "I'd like another cup, please". The alternatives "shut up" and "be silent, please" mark different personal tenors.

MARKED: (See *Marker*.)

MAJOR CLAUSE: A clause which contains a predicator. "Bring me coffee, please" is a major clause because it contains the predicator "Bring". (See *Minor clause*.)

MINOR CLAUSE: A clause without a predicator. "Coffee, please" is a minor clause because it has no predicator. (See *Major clause*.)

MODE OF DISCOURSE: The division of language at lowest delicacy into two varieties: spoken language and written language. Under spoken, at higher delicacy, we distinguish between spontaneous and nonspontaneous speech. Spontaneous speech may be divided into two categories, conversing and monologuing; nonspontaneous, into reciting (for instance, schoolyard rhymes), and "speaking what is written" (for example, the lines of a play or a speech read aloud from a script). Written language may be divided into three categories: "written to be spoken as if not written", "written to be spoken", and "written not necessarily to be spoken". Writing is, of course, a relatively recent development in man's history. Even today, most of the more than 8,000 languages known exist only in the spoken mode. Even in our culture, children acquire the essentials of grammar while they are operating entirely within the spoken mode.

MODIFIER: Any element occurring before the head in the structure of a nominal group. Examples are the group "my hat", with one modifier plus head, and the group "the six best old china plates", with five modifiers plus head. (See *Group structure*.)

MONOLOGUING: Spontaneous speech which does not invite participation by others; for example, an extemporaneous sermon. (See *Mode of discourse*.)

MORPHEME: The unit of English grammar ranked below the word. Morphemes are the units which typically make up words. Morphemes are at the bottom of the rank scale; there are no smaller grammatical units which make them up. The word "gives" is made up of two morphemes: "give" and "s". The word "man" is made up of one morpheme, "man". The word "manhood" is made up of two morphemes: "man" and "hood". The word "men" is made up of two morphemes: "man" and the internal change in form to "men". The word "unknown" is made up of three morphemes: "un", "know", and "n". (See *Word*.)

NARRATION: A category of functional tenor. Narration describes past or present events, usually in chronological order. A history book will contain a great deal of narrative. So will a sports announcer's broadcast of a hockey game.

NOMINAL GROUP: The kind of group which can typically operate as subject element or complement element in the structure of a clause. "John" and "cake" in "John eats cake", "The red house" in "The red house blew down", and both "He" and "the slightly rancid bacon" in "He ate the slightly rancid bacon" are nominal groups. (See *Group structure*.)

PERSONAL TENOR: The degree of formality of a text, measured on a scale from informal to formal. "My old man" is definitely informal; "Dad" is somewhere in the middle; and "Father" is near the formal end of the scale. (See *Diatypic varieties*.)

PERSUASION: A category of functional tenor. Most advertising is persuasive language. (See *Functional tenor*.)

PHATIC COMMUNION: A category of functional tenor. Phatic communion is language which establishes a sense of personal contact and a feeling of good will between the speakers. Much of the small talk at parties, and the opening remarks made by people when they meet are phatic communion. (See *Functional tenor*.)

PHONETICS: The study of the sound originating in the human vocal tract.

PHONETIC TRANSCRIPTION: An attempt to record by symbols, which by convention are enclosed in square brackets, as many features of the sound of an utterance as can be distinguished. [pʰ] is a transcription of the "p" at the beginning of a word. It is a sound different from [p], the "p" which follows "s" in a word.

PHONOLOGY: The study of the organization in a particular language of the sounds produced by the human vocal tract. Phonology recognizes /p/ as meaningful in English; phonetics, but not phonology, is interested in the fact that the "p" in "pit" is aspirated, while that in "spit" is not. Phonology establishes the existence of the phoneme /p/ in English by contrasting it with other sounds. A native English speaker would recognize "pit" as different in meaning from "bit"; /p/ and /b/ are therefore different phonemes.

PREDICATOR: One of the five elements of clause structure. It is always a verbal group, and often follows the subject. Examples are "ran" in the clause "She ran", and "may be being chased", in the clause "She may be being chased". (See *Group structure*.)

PURPOSIVE ROLE: The interest of the speaker reflected in his field of discourse. If the purposive role of a speaker is to explain mathematics, for example, he is likely to use the lexical items "plus", "minus", "product", "sine", etc., and graphologically to produce the symbols √ and x. (See *Field of discourse*.)

QUALIFIER: Any element occurring after the head in the structure of a nominal group. "On the table" in the group "the glass on the table", and "who love cats" in the group "people who love cats" are qualifiers. (See *Group structure*.)

RANK SCALE: The hierarchy of inclusiveness of units. From least inclusive to most inclusive, the five units in English grammar are: morpheme, word, group, clause, and sentence. Normally each unit is made up of one or more of the units of the rank below it. For example, the sentence "My uncle might like my sister, but he hates me" is made up of two clauses. The first of these clauses is made up of three groups: "My uncle", "might like", and "my sister". The first of these groups is made up of two words: "My" and "uncle". The word "hates" is made up of two morphemes: "hate" and "s". (See *Rankshift* for the exception to this general rule.)

RANKSHIFT: In grammatical structure, the replacement of any normal unit by a unit ranked *above* it. For example, the group "the/only/chair/available" exhibits normal structure: each element (modifier, head, qualifier) is a word. In the group "the/only/chair/ with a leather back" the qualifier is itself a group. "With a leather back" is thus a group within the structure of a group. Since it is higher on the rank scale than the normal unit, word, it is rankshifted. In the group "the/only/chair/he liked", the qualifier is a clause. "He liked" is thus a clause within the structure of a group. Since a clause, like a group, is higher on the rank scale than the normal unit, word, it too is rankshifted. Rankshift occurs frequently in clauses. For example, the clause "Fried fish/is/a great dinner", comprised of three groups, contrasts with "What I want/is/a great dinner". In this form a rankshifted clause, "what I want" replaces the normal unit (group).

RECITING: The speaking exactly of material learned from an unwritten source. Schoolyard taunts are familiar examples. An actor's rendition of a play is not in this mode because his lines have been learned from a written source. (See *Mode of discourse*.)

SENTENCE: A grammatical unit which is not a part of a larger grammatical unit. *From Here to Eternity*, the title of the novel, is not part of a larger grammatical unit, and is therefore a sentence. In "I shall run from here to eternity", the same four words form part of a larger unit and do not, therefore, constitute a sentence. Sentences do not always contain verbs, although they often do.

SET: (See *Lexical set*.)

SITUATION: That part of a language phenomenon's environment which is relevant to the language. For example, a sign reading "dangerous current" could be found in different environments: on the wall of a power generating station or by a swiftly flowing river. Whether or not the generating station is coal fired or oil fired is irrelevant to linguistic situation. What is situationally relevant is that the sign is on a generating station, and not by a river bank, because this is what unambiguously makes the field of discourse "electricity" rather than "water flow". Situation consists, of course, of more than physical setting. Such internal factors as a speaker's mood, intention and the like are clearly relevant to his language. Both internal and external factors are constantly changing, and a speaker's language reflects these differing situations. He will, for example, speak differently to his mother, his girl friend, or the milkman. Or, with any of these, he will speak differently if he is angry or relaxed. He will speak differently if using a telephone. His language will change even more if the person is not present and there is no telephone. In this case, situation will result in a change of mode — he will write.

SOCIAL DIALECT: The language spoken by a distinct class of people. For example, Shakespeare's rustics as opposed to his aristocratic characters.

SPONTANEOUS SPEECH: Spoken language in which the lexical and grammatical choices are made extemporaneously. "Spontaneous" does not imply that the subject is not known in great detail. Sometimes it is, as when a speaker has a very full outline of what he is going to say. (See *Mode of discourse*.)

SUBJECT: One of the five elements of clause structure. It usually occurs immediately before the predicator, or immediately after the first word of the predicator. For example, "I" in "I like old films", or "the film" in "Was the film interesting?". Note that a "subject" is an element of clause structure, and not of sentence structure.

SYSTEM: A fixed and limited number of possibilities from which a language user must choose. Grammar, phonology, and graphology describe systems.

TEMPORAL DIALECT: The variety of language spoken at a particular time. Language changes during the course of time. Middle English, for example, differs grammatically and lexically from Modern English. At low delicacy, Mark Twain and William Faulkner both write in the temporal dialect Modern English. At greater delicacy, their temporal dialects may be shown to differ.

TEXT: The stretch of language, written or spoken, under consideration at a given time.

UNIT: A stretch of language which carries structural pattern. For example, the three following stretches of language, "He chopped the tree", "Lemons taste sour", and "Existentialism is complicated", all contain the same pattern: subject, predicator, and complement. Such units are called *clauses*. Similarly "old men with beards", "Bright colours on canvas", and "jumbo jets full of passengers", can all be seen to contain the same pattern: modifier, head, and qualifier. Such units are called *groups*. The other units of English grammar are *sentence*, *word*, and *morpheme*. (See *Rank scale*.)

VARIETY: A particular type of language. Linguistic study makes it evident that there is no one "English language". Under the category of mode, for instance, we describe written and spoken English, which are distinct from each other. The purpose of this book is to demonstrate that there are many varieties of English.

VERBAL GROUP: A group which can act as predicator in the structure of a clause. Examples are: "loves" in "She loves him", "is going to be chosen" in "She is going to be

WORD:

chosen", and "ought to cut" in "He ought to cut down the tree". (See *Group structure.*)

The unit of English grammar ranked below the group. A word is typically made up of morphemes, and makes up groups. "Unlovely" in the group "my unlovely cook" is a word made up of three morphemes: "un", "love", and "ly". It is one of three words which make up the group. (See *Group structure* and *Morpheme.*)

Z ELEMENT:

One of the five elements of clause structure: a nominal group which is not overtly related to a predicator. It may be that there is no predicator, as, for example, the clause "Tickets, please", in which "Tickets" is a Z element and "please" is an adjunct. Sometimes, even when there is a predicator, there is also a nominal group which is not directly related to it. In "Mr. Jones, I love you", "Mr. Jones" is a Z element. (See *Clause structure.*)